Something Should Be Said

A Memoir of Five Abandoned Children

Laura P. Dye

Copyright © 2021 Laura P. Dye

ISBN: 9798460598427

All rights reserved. No portion of this book may be reproduced in any form without permission from the publisher, except as permitted by U.S. copyright law. For permissions contact: laurapdye@gmail.com

Design: Roger Dye

Cover Background by Steve Johnson from Pexels

Illustration of Girl with Chickens: Stockunlimited

Dedicated to five precious children.

Contents

Foreword 1
Mundane Treasures 5
Say It 9
Saying It In Court 11
Personal Reasons 13
Little Girl Arrives 19
The Boxes 25
Let's Tell This Story 27
Baltic Germans 31
Nani and Pop's Immigration 35
Mildred and Reece 37
Galveston 41
June 15, 1945 47
Compassion 51
The Baby Who Cried All the Time 55
We Ran Away 61
Miss McCombs 63

Little Girl in the Bathtub 67

Life at DePelchin Faith Home 69

Cabbages 75

The Blessing of Faith Home 79

About Foster Homes 81

Daddy's Home! 85

Little Girl Perched 91

Mother 93

I Hurt Her 101

Electric and Extraordinary! 103

The House at Delafield 109

Grandmother's Husbands 117

Scrubbed Clean 123

The Sewage Grate 129

The Kind People 133

Joe Euresti and Others 139

Reprieve? 143

Pine Tree Camp 145

Dena 151

Rage, Grace and Mercy 155

Foreword

My mother and her four siblings had an unusual childhood growing up under the care of DePelchin Faith Home in Houston, Texas. They were in and out of foster homes and their parents' homes. At best it could be called "difficult." At worst, "abusive." None of it can be fixed with a few words on pages but it can be spoken out loud that this was not good and the loss they suffered was profound. I feel privileged to have been allowed into their lives, to shed some tears, and to have an education in the pain of selfish wrongs inflicted on innocent children.

This is a grieving book. I (and you, if you'd like) grieve the losses the children were never allowed to grieve or even mention. The loss of the family unit, protection, and innocence were their experience when their childhood should have included deep love in the context of family. I wonder who they would have been without all that they endured. I wonder. I cannot possibly plumb the depths of their pain nor express how remarkable their childhood was. And it was as remarkable as it was painful.

Finally, I should probably mention something about the writing style. I guess I'll call it ADHD-memoir style. As I was writing, I thought I really should be more organized, but my mind is not organized in the normal way. I do believe that comes straight from my delightful Momma. Her mind flitted around in the loveliest of ways. My siblings and I could always change the subject, and she flew like a bird with us.

So, I ask you to hang on while my mind flies to multiple places, past and present, through the chaotic foster system of the 1940's and 50', to a short visit to a Chilean orphanage and on an occasional fast forward to 21st century foster care with our precious Little Girl. Buckle up for a roller coaster ride through chaos, the world many foster children still live in today.

Chapter 1

Mundane Treasures

Demure, deep-set, blue-gray eyes, sad, smiling, gentle, confused yet understanding. She combed her dark curls around her beautiful face and removed the black pearls from her jewelry box. If I had known the word, I would have called her black sheath dress sexy. I rested my chin on the smooth dresser and watched her, sneaking my fingers into the other "jewels" in the box. She snapped the box closed and smiled the gentle sweet smile I hold in a special place in my memory. It was the kind of smile that said, "You are my perfect little girl, and I love you."

I spun around on the bar stool. Momma rolled out the pie crust and carefully placed it on the pie pan. My eyes learned as quickly as I could how to make a basket weave on a pie. I asked how to make it, and she showed me how to use a fork and knife to break up the flour, salt, and shortening mixture and turn it into a crust. My arms hurt and I was frustrated. She encouraged me that it would come together if I would work patiently.

She hung the clothes on the line. After she finished, I walked through the white sheets and rubbed my face on the wet cloth. There were not many ways to get cool on a hot summer day. She let me do it.

These everyday memories seem mundane, not much to write about except that I loved her so much and miss her now that she is gone. The mundane that tucked me into bed each night with the song, "Father we thank Thee for the night, and for the pleasant morning light, for rest and food and clothes we wear, and all that makes the world so fair. Amen." She leaned down to hug and kiss me and let me hold onto her for more.

It's hard for me to believe and perhaps even impossible that this beautiful, loving creature who nurtured me in the truest sense of the word didn't offer these mundane treasures from her own experience. Her experience involved watching a wide belt strike her mother's back as her father expressed his rage at her mother's infidelity. Poverty and messy divorce landed eight-year-old demure eyes on the front porch of The DePelchin Faith Home.

Her mother just left her.

Surely Grandmother cried. Surely she missed her. Surely she couldn't sleep for longing for this little girl.

In my mind I always saw my mother at Faith Home alone or with one of her sisters. My mouth dropped open when Aunt Sandy, sister number three, shook her head, "No." All five kids were left at DePelchin Faith Home at one time. All five children: Deanna "Dena" Lee (my mother), Lena Marie, Sandra Maurine, Jimmie Lou and David Morris Brooks. Momma was eight. Uncle David was a baby. Aunt Sandy said, "I think I cried for months." She had no idea that her mother wasn't coming back until she didn't come back.

She didn't come back.

I once saw Momma and Aunt Sandy say "goodbye" to each other as adults. It was different with them than with other sisters. They had a little language of their own that no one else understood. Even I didn't get it. They hugged and held each other while tears poured, the kind of tears that children shed when they aren't supposed to cry: quiet, sorrowful and sad. I was watching two little girls being ripped apart all over again... all over again. But Aunt Sandy was just traveling back to Texas to be with her children and grandchildren. They never got used to the abandonment and shuffling from foster homes, abusive caregivers, and back into Faith Home. More than seventy-five years later, it still hurts.

Mom's parents were ordered by a judge to make their marriage work, for the sake of the children, but my grandfather's resentment and my grandmother's brokenness hardened them both. As soft and gentle as my mother was, Grandmother was hard. My grandparents set about working on the marriage, taking dance classes together. It never worked. Their marriage, instead of cultivating any sort of love, bred hatred and revenge. They pummeled each other and killed the life inside their five children. But those children were tough. They fought everyone in Faith Home, ran away, cried, and screamed, until they were broken. Until the life went out in each one, replaced by things I do not understand.

Chapter 2

Say It

I read the previous chapter to Aunt Sandy while she awaited a heart catheterization in the hospital. Her eyes were now dry and mine were wet. Okay, so I was blubbering! I wanted her approval, but I didn't want to hurt her by telling the story. I asked her what she thought. She didn't even have to think. She said, "It just feels good to have someone say it." My emotions roared. Something should be said. I could do that.

As I reflect on the naked truth of horrors selfishly inflicted on innocent ones, I realize that I placed the blame squarely on my grandparents' shoulders and much of that rests on Grandmother. Grandmother never admitted regret to anyone, ever. And those children desperately needed her to regret it.

Even though they tried, the kids were never allowed to speak about the abandonment, even as adults. Grandmother never "said it" and those kids desperately needed her, of all people, to "say it." It is indeed small for me to "say it" now, but something should be said.

Chapter 3

Saying It In Court

As a missionary wife standing beside my husband, Roger, as he speaks is one of the greatest joys I have, but today it took on new importance. Today he spoke in family court of our observations of the effects of abuse and neglect on our foster child, Little Girl. His voice was soft and careful, but I could see the goosebumps on his forearms as he measured the words and their importance to a helpless one's future. This almost seven-year-old couldn't count to two. She was malnourished and lacked language because of isolation. The words of adult survivors of abuse, in particular Momma and her siblings spur us on to "say it" whether or not anyone listens.

So Roger said it.

The mother bowed her head while the translator relayed our accusations. The judge thanked us for our service as foster parents. I didn't want the thanks unless he was going to protect this precious one who called me "Tia" and sometimes "Chicken Nugget.," (Don't ask me why because I have no idea.) Maybe they listened some but probably not nearly as much as we wanted. An extra few sessions were added to family counseling. God knew and had hemmed our Little Girl in before and behind. It's enough to let her rest a little while longer in our arms.

Chapter 4

Personal Reasons

Roger and I lived and worked in Viña del Mar, Chile as church planting missionaries for about sixteen years. In our first few years there, our colleagues, John and Cathy Rug had connected with a girls' home in Valparaiso, the port city just a short twenty-minute drive from our home. John is blind and taught at the school for the blind where they met a little girl named Juanita. Juanita who is visually impaired, lived in the orphanage. John and Cathy began fostering her on weekends, working towards the difficult process of adopting Juanita. Her little dark head bounced as she skipped and ran through the Rug home. She brought her two pairs of shoes and danced around. When I go out, I put on my regular shoes and then I put on my *pantuflas* or slippers. (I like the word *pantuflas*, pronounced "pahn-too-flahs" with an emphasis and lilt on the "too".) She was in heaven and John and Cathy were *chochos* (overflowing with happiness) in loving this little girl who had blessed them (and us) every day since they met her. We got the overspill watching with joy as Juanita, who called me Aunt Laura, became a Rug. We knew the process was complete when she exclaimed in the midst of her little-girl Spanish, "Wowza!" Yeah, she was a Rug for sure. Juanita was enchanting.

We certainly tried to be supportive of the girls in the orphanage. Our family attended a Christmas program at the girls' home. After the program, a woman pulled me aside and told me that for Christmas almost all the girls go stay in a relative's home. Two sisters had no place to go. Would we like to take them for a long weekend? Of course, we would love to have them! We weren't looking forward to Christmas far from our family anyway. I quickly bought a small dollhouse for one of the girls and a something else for the younger sister. I don't even remember what I bought, but our lonely Christmas turned into something else very quickly.

We picked the girls up and made our first stop at John and Cathy Rug's home. They had more experience with the special circumstances that accompanied these girls: lice, and lots of them. Cathy combed the lice out of both girls' hair while I watched a bit helplessly. The caregivers at the home had cut the girls' hair short so at least that part was easy. The bugs were big and healthy and ran all over the girls. All over! They say that the most neglected girls have the most lice. These two were certainly in that category. So, all cleaned up, they came along to our home. Our children played and laughed through most of the visit.

Christmas morning was everything you would want it to be: children running in pajamas, squealing with delight. We did discover that the dollhouse we'd bought was not a dollhouse at all, but doll furniture for a dollhouse so Roger spent Christmas morning building a dollhouse out of cardboard. That was disappointing, but it was probably better than having a dollhouse already built. Roger spent precious time with a girl who was hard as hard could be. She melted just a wee bit with patient Roger beside her. The biggest melting happened when the girls took a bubble bath. I hope someday you have the privilege of giving a little girl a bubble bath who has never had that experience. It was the best!!

At one point we visited Juanita's orphanage. Momma and Daddy had come to visit us and joined us in our Hyundai "tin can van," climbing the *cerros* (hills) of Valparaiso up cobblestoned streets winding and winding until we reached a little flat street. We parked just beside the orphanage. It was a large old home from the 1920s perhaps, refitted as an orphanage. I don't say "renovated" because there were few improvements from its original construction. The caregivers just moved in with a bunch of little girls.

The rumbly sidewalks showed years of earthquakes that hadn't quite destroyed them yet. It just made them a bumpy, hilly nightmare for a blind man. Just a few steps and we entered through the old double doors and then another set of doors designed to keep the cool wet breeze from entering the house. It was dark, but we could see. A distinct salad-dressing smell filled the air. The caregivers were trying to get a handle on the terrible lice problem that plagued all the little girls. Their home remedy was oil and vinegar and a plastic bag on the girls' heads. We weren't sure it really works, but at least they were trying. Happy little girls ran around dripping with the smell of salad.

Momma was not smiling.

I was pretty sure this was the first orphanage Momma had ever been inside of since her own childhood at Faith Home. She looked around as Juanita shows her where she slept and the bathroom. All the little girls had been given Barbie dolls the previous week. Cathy chuckled as she caught a glimpse of every single one of the dolls hanging by their necks outside on the clothesline with clothes nowhere in sight. Momma looked around at the mounds of communal clothes. Her eyes fell on a pile of stockings, and it was hard to tell if they were clean or not. Cathy whispers that they were "crunchy."

Momma said, "We had our own things." She took a few more steps. "We each had our own little cubbyhole for our things," she explained shifting her focus to Juanita instead of what she considered deplorable conditions for children to live in.

John and Cathy had at least snatched one little girl out of that place, and we were joyful just watching Juanita giggle and learn what family now means to her.

Later, in the quiet of the evening, Momma and I sat down for a cup of tea. She questioned why we would get involved in such a work. "Is it because of me?" she said. Well, yeah! Of course it was because of Momma. Her response was, "Well, don't." Hearing that from a mom who never told me what to do or how to do it regarding our work or family I took her words very seriously.

We actually stopped working with the orphanage almost as soon as we began but the thought that we ought to be doing something always stayed with me. I see my mom being left at the orphanage and my heart is in shreds. Yes, it was because of Momma that I wanted to do something, anything, to alleviate the pain of a child who could very well have been my own mother.

Now that she is gone, we have gotten involved deeply with fostering in the US. I know that Mom's reasoning behind her very clear mandate was that she wanted us as far away from and out of "the system" as possible. "Ward of the State" was the title she hated the most. She never wanted us to even have a whiff of social services air on our clothes. Now that I stink like our dysfunctional Department of Social Services, I understand… a little.

When we returned to the US permanently, we met Little Girl, our first foster child. Reunification is the goal of almost all foster situations. Little Girl was no different, but we have seen firsthand what cruel, bad or no parenting can do to a person and how it changes who they are. We have seen a little girl thriving under what we consider normal circumstances: food, education, safety.

I think of my aunt's longing as a young girl for her parents to release their parental rights so that she could have been happy, but they never let any of the kids be adopted. They were kept in a cage so to speak. It was cruel.

Perhaps we can be very intentional about seeing that Little Girl's family never has influence over her. We can make sure she never has to go back to that. Maybe with the help of a lawyer?

Then I remember.

I love my aunts and uncle and how thankful I am to have them in my life. For them their sibling group is everything! Everything. Then I wonder, was it worth it? Was it worth it to live in chaos and abuse to keep their precious family together, sort of?

Okay, so we want it all. We want our family, and we want it to be safe and nurturing. Why should children have to choose

CHAPTER 5

Little Girl Arrives

Some parents tell their children about the day they were born. This is the story we told Little Girl who says that we are "almost old" about the day she arrived at our home... her home:

Había una vez una mujer casi viejita y un hombre casi viejito. Ella comenzó a hacer galletas mientras el hombre casi viejito fue a trabajar. Llego un auto blanco con una niña atrás durmiendo con su unicornio. La niña abrió sus ojos cafés bajo el cabello negro y sonrió una sonrisa como un rayo de sol, aunque no tenia muchos dientes

La mujer casi viejita invito a la niña preciosa a entrar a la casa. El unicornio dormía mientras la niña preciosa y la mujer casi viejita salieron a buscar los huevos de gallina.

Abrieron la casa de las gallinas con mucho cuidado, pero igual se asustó una gallina. La niña preciosa y la mujer casi viejita se rieron mucho mientras recolectaban los huevos cafés y azules. Los pusieron en una canasta y los llevaron a la casa. Juntas hicieron galletas hasta que el hombre casi viejito llego del trabajo.

Cuando él vio a la niña preciosa, exclamo susurrando, "¿Crees que tenemos una cama para ella?" La mujer casi viejita dijo, "¡Sí, tenemos una cama perfecta para ella!"

Y la mujer casi viejita y el hombre casi viejito amaron a la niña preciosa con un amor muy fuerte.

Once upon a time there was an almost-old woman and an almost-old man. She began to make cookies while the almost-old man went to work. A white car arrived with a little girl sleeping in the backseat with her unicorn. The little girl opened her brown eyes beneath her black hair and smiled a smile as bright as sunshine, even though she didn't have many teeth.

The almost-old woman invited the precious girl to come inside the house. The little white unicorn napped while the precious girl and the almost old woman went outside to gather eggs.

They opened the chicken coop very carefully, but frightened a poor hen just the same. The precious girl and the almost-old woman laughed and laughed while they gathered the blue and brown eggs. They placed them in a basket and brought them inside the house. The almost-old woman and the precious girl made cookies together until the almost-old man came home from work.

When he saw the precious girl, he exclaimed whispering, "Do you think we have a bed for her?" The almost-old woman said, "Yes! We have the perfect bed for her!"

And the almost-old woman and the almost-old man loved the precious girl with a very strong love.

"Okay Tia. Now you gonna tell me how they get the babies out."

Most of us found ourselves sputtering at one time or another with Little Girl but this time was, well… I kind of felt like this was an interrogation. I was either going to talk or something terrible would happen. I had no idea what it would be, but it would be terrible.

We had reluctantly decided to let Little Girl read books and fall asleep in our bed with me and then move her to her bed. With her recurring nightmares and fears we felt like it was best for our whole family not to be awake past midnight each night. This particular night, Roger read books to us, prayed, and then walked out, closing the door. Little Girl quickly got down to business. I had averted the question in the car that afternoon but she had not forgotten. She wanted to know!

"Okay, Tia. Now you gonna tell me how they get the babies out." I sputtered that I thought that would be something she could talk about with her mom. No, her face fell, giving me the litmus test of where she stood with her mom. So I made something up, all true but certainly more of a blurred version for a seven-year-old than the full truth.

This is what I get. This is what I get for going against what they told me. They told me not to fall in love. It is fostering, temporary, guard your heart. But ever since the Department of Social Services intern drove up the driveway in her white SUV and showed me a little slip of a girl with dark hair over her brown eyes, sound asleep. She woke up and smiled at me a toothless grin, I fell hard. It's amazing how quickly our hearts can get entangled. So there I sat, almost a year later, entangled with a precious girl who now had a full smile and wanted me to tell her how they get the babies out.

It seems to have nothing to do with writing about Momma and our family, DePelchin Faith Home or anything except that we were just about to send her back into her family, the family who didn't teach a seven-year-old how to count to two. We had the power to love her well for a year, but I am certain it was not enough.

Did someone feel like that about my Momma? Did someone look into those deep-set blue eyes and dare to absorb some of her sadness? Did someone burn with anger at what my grandmother was doing, or not doing, to her children by her immaturity? Did another woman cry inside that Momma had lost her mother in the worst of ways, the way where her mother was still there but she wasn't there. The sorrow of loss that isn't really loss is the worst kind. To have a mother and be unable to embrace her, to lack the love of a mother and not be allowed another mother to love her, is unbearably cruel.

Chapter 6

The Boxes

The boxes scare me. Momma has been gone for years now and many papers, boxes, journals and notes have been thrown away or tucked away for the precious truth contained. Momma stored them all neatly in stacks in the storehouse. Cleaning out the storehouse was the last of the chores to close up Mom and Dad's estate.

The storehouse was built probably before the 1925 companion house where I now live. It is old and has dodged almost a hundred years of tornados, hurricane Hugo in 1989, termites and who knows how many country dogs that have lived underneath it or mice that have enjoyed the cardboard storage boxes left to age like wine in the steaming South Carolina heat. It has always looked friendly to me. As children we always looked around carefully before we rummaged through the very interesting things. It did not look friendly to me today.

The ancient weather-beaten door creaked open and the chain let go of it, dropping and rattling on the door frame. It's not like we never looked in the storehouse. We were quite familiar with its contents and the old, old things inside. In the back an old bucket hung from the ceiling. It was used for drawing water from the well before my dad's parents, Grandmother and Granddaddy had the windmill. That was a long time ago!

It was the stack of Momma's boxes marked Dena's journals that sickened both my sister and me. You'd think we would be happy to see more words written by our dear Mom's hand but we knew our sometimes tormented mother recorded every detail. She always spared us such details in her life but here they were in a stack of boxes, concentrated pain and torture, prayers, verses all interspersed with lists about green beans, bluebird nests, robins and my waist measurements from 1976. Also tucked inside were a stray lock of her hair, my hair, and ribbon from a corsage with what she described as "the most beautiful white orchid I have ever seen."

She also recorded the sweetness of things around her, of our anecdotes as children, the birds and then more birds followed by exactly how God comforted, carried her even in the good times. Her songs in the night were my favorite. God carried her and she knew it well. Yet to open the boxes and pore over her life before she got to the place of contentment is a hard thing to think about. My sister and I agreed to dump them in the gulley and closed the door.

I never dumped them. These last few years I have pulled out pieces here and there to see what exactly the boxes contain. If she protected us from so much, why did she save it all for us? To understand? Her journaling and note-taking were obsessive, compulsive; she had to write something down.

She protected us. I will think about that as I decide how deep to go into the boxes and how much to share. My initial thought is to share oh so little because it isn't necessary and no doubt it will hurt…us.

Chapter 7

Let's Tell This Story

Everyone I know has some sort of immigration story. Even if it's only the confession of being from Scotch-Irish roots, we all have a story because we all came from somewhere else, not South Carolina and not Texas. Very few hold the heritage of being original inhabitants of any soil in the US. We all came from somewhere.

My father tells the story of the Park family. We came from Scotland by way of Ireland never intermarrying. Apparently that was a big deal not to marry an Irish national for perhaps centuries while our people resided in Ireland. Not that there is no Irish blood, but during that period of time our family didn't intermarry. It speaks of the stubbornness of my people, their tenacity, the terrible conditions that must have prevailed to motivate them to leave their home and pass through a people group that I gather they found distasteful, at least distasteful enough to be proud enough not to consider them appropriate marriage partners. Note that I don't say this with pride, but amusement. It is amusing to think that our family was so closed-minded and that their stubbornness persisted until the year 1962 when Daddy fell in love with a beautiful girl of

Puerto Rican and Latvian heritage with some other British genes by way of Texas floating around.

The blood of my father's ancestors runs through my veins so I shouldn't smirk at it. As traditional as Daddy's side of the family was, my great grandmother Park did have some rogue instincts enough to marry a man unapproved by her father, though he was still in the clans. Perhaps the opportunity to marry outside the clans didn't avail itself until 1962 when Daddy was working far from home in White Sands Desert, New Mexico. Perhaps. But he was twitterpated, head over heels, blinded to the family gene that told him to be careful, conservative, calculate the risks. His love blindness was coupled with a sense that what was good might not be the way the family had always done it. Leon McCants Park married Deanna Lee Brooks.

His comment to me when my husband and I married after a short courtship of a few months was, "Well, you will just have a few more surprises." He was speaking from experience. The more I learn, the more thankful I am that Momma married a tenacious man of Scottish heritage, who, for all his faults and shortcomings, refused to give up on the woman he was so in love with in 1962. As in all marriages, the qualities that most intrigue us about our partners become the qualities that most irritate us, if not handled in love. Their marriage flourished despite their different backgrounds. It was a rocky road, but all of us kids remember catching the two of them embracing in the kitchen. Even the last year of their lives together, Momma caressed Daddy's Parkinson's ridden face and he responded,"Did I tell you that you are really good?"

Daddy's history gives me insight into where my red hair and blue eyes came from. It gives me an excuse to be stubborn and traditional. Perhaps telling parts of Momma's family and immigration history might give us some insight into what caused people I would consider reasonable to do things that no reasonable person would ever dream of doing. No reasonable person would from one day to the next place five children in the care of an orphanage unless many other factors forced them into such impossible decisions. Surely there are explanations in her history.

Chapter 8

Baltic Germans

To tell a complete family history means to thoroughly study and investigate historically as far back as we can go. Various relatives on both sides of my family have done that already. Instead, I will focus on a few people whom I find interesting and whom I believe had a huge role in Momma's life long before she was ever born, long before the decisions that led to what Aunt Lena calls "her sentence" in Faith Home. Here is one part of our family's immigration story.

August Knipps was my great-grandfather, Pop. I never met him but he immigrated from Latvia in the early part of the 1900's. He was born in Latvia which was part of Russia at that time, but he always claimed to be German. That was a mystery to me until I read an article like this Wikipedia entry about Baltic Germans in Latvia:

> The Baltic Germans... are ethnic German inhabitants of the eastern shores of the Baltic Sea, in what today are Estonia and Latvia. In the 12th and 13th centuries Catholic Germans, both traders and crusaders (see Ostsiedlung), began settling in the eastern Baltic territories.
>
> After the Livonian Crusade, they assumed control of government, politics, economics, education and culture of

> these lands, ruling for more than 700 years until 1918 — usually in alliance with Polish, Swedish or Russian overlords. With the decline of Latin, German became the language of all official documents, commerce, education and government.
>
> At first the majority of German settlers lived in small cities and military castles. Their elite formed the Baltic nobility, acquiring large rural estates and comprising the social, commercial, political and cultural elite of Latvia and Estonia for several centuries. After 1710 many of these men increasingly took high positions in the military, political and civilian life of the Russian Empire, particularly in Saint Petersburg. Baltic Germans held citizenship in the Russian Empire until the Revolution of 1918. They then held Estonian or Latvian citizenship until the occupation and later annexation of these areas by the Soviet Union in 1939–1940.

For Pop, being German was a declaration of class as well as an ethnicity! To be just Latvian would make him a commoner in an intricate class system where the upper class of nobility had position and power, albeit crumbling before his very eyes. It explains why he called himself German. He was German. Even though that ethnicity could go well back to the thirteenth century, he held onto that heritage. His family could very well have been in Latvia for centuries. Pop's mother was ethnically Latvian but the family held on tightly to the German ethnicity.

Pop told Aunt Jennifer that he was from Talsi, a place with nine hills. Another relative understood that Pop was from Riga, the largest city in Latvia situated on the Port of Riga. Talsi is just west of Riga so I wonder if it could be that he identified himself with both places. Peering into the unfamiliar landscape of Latvia it looks pleasant and hospitable, yet he left it all. It was certainly a different time. The "nobility" was crumbling and Pop would be faced with some very difficult decisions.

It was the end of the German ruling class in Latvia. Russia fought a series of battles across Lithuania and Latvia (part of the Bolshevik Revolution), March 8-18, 1917 and again November 7-8, 1917. In the late 1800's the Germans had already aligned themselves with Russia politically and were seen as traitors by the German empire. Baltic Germans had to make a choice between Russia or Germany. If Pop were indeed a Baltic German, he would have had to make an impossible choice. In 1905 Pop's parents encouraged him to leave (or flee) before he no longer had any choice. He found himself on a ship and then in the merchant marines. Pop immigrated to the US.

He worked odd jobs for a time until he became the captain of a lighthouse tender. The ship sailed from Nova Scotia to the Caribbean, refilling the storage tanks of whale oil that kept the lighthouses supplied.

Apparently Pop liked the Puerto Rico stop. He married a Puerto Rican woman. She died and he married her cousin, my great-grandmother Monserrat Pabon, who is affectionately known as Nani. Nani came from Spanish and Italian heritage: the Pabon family. Her father was the mayor of his town in Cabo Rojo.

Nani was a beauty. Even when she was an old woman they spoke of her beauty and her sweetness. She married Pop and their little family began.

Chapter 9

Nani and Pop's Immigration

Pop had already immigrated to the US by way of Ship Island, Mississippi. Nani, my great-grandmother, came by way of Ellis Island and settled in Norfolk, VA with my grandmother, Mildred May, almost three years old, Great-Aunt Gladys fifteen months, Great-Uncle Joe was two months and Great-Uncle Bill was born in Virginia. After many years as a merchant marine living on ships, Pop was diagnosed with tuberculosis around 1929. There was no cure for TB then, but with the completion of the railroad, many were encouraged to look for healing in the dry warm climate of the Southwest. Pop went to Fort Bayard, New Mexico.

My grandmother wrote:

> We children were separated because our Pop went to Fort Bayard, NM to be treated for tuberculosis. My sister, smaller brother and I lived in an orphanage in Norfolk, Virginia while my mother worked in the laundry to support us. My older brother was sent to an orphanage in Roanoke, Virginia. We are Catholic at the time. These orphanages were run by the Catholic Sisters. In 1929 my mother went to live in the area where my father was and took our small brother with her. She later sent for my sister and me and we

> lived with a young lady in New Mexico where we went to school. We later (1 yr) were placed in an orphanage, (Methodist), in El Paso, Texas where our mother worked and lived. My father was still in Fort Bayard but becoming an arrested case and would move to El Paso. In 1932, we were all together again at 2312 Pittsburgh St, in El Paso.

Although Grandmother wrote with a factual crispness, there are places we can see how painful it was for the family. "We children were separated..." and then the mention of orphanages, three of them. Her mother wasn't too far and the time periods weren't too long, but I am sure it marked her and the whole family. By the time Grandmother had written this terse history she had already calloused over that painful spot, chalking it up to the way things were in those days. Of course she had to be bounced around and the family separated some. Her father was sick with a deadly disease and no known cure. The kids needed to understand the necessity of flexing with the family.

It was in the midst of parents making desperate decisions that a precedent for using orphanages was set. When Grandmother had trouble, DePelchin Faith Home became a viable option.

Chapter 10

Mildred and Reece

Nani and Pop lived in El Paso with their children. What led to the vacation in Galveston, Texas, I don't know. At this point because the rest of this story can be so damning to someone, mostly Grandmother, I'll let her tell how she came to meet and marry my grandfather, Jody Maurice Brooks. There are questions around that meeting, but here is how Grandmother, or Mildred, explained it in a document she intended to give clarity to their history:

> "At my father's request, I went along with Mom on a trip to Galveston, Texas, in May, 1936. I still had to finish High School by virtue that I had a full load in my second and third year of High School. I met a young man the first day. My father decided to come down and enjoy the sea so this man said I could stay in his room at night, because he was working from 7 pm - 7 am. He asked me to marry him but wait until I finished school the next year. My parents talked and I was married one week from the day I met this man."

I furrow my brow and wonder what in the world is going on?! What were they thinking? Even if the two "kids" were anxious and willing to marry, wouldn't parents put the brakes on the idea at least for a month, or a year?

Granddaddy told his mother, Mama Brooks, "They want me to marry Mildred."

Apparently he did, too. According to my grandmother's family, when it came time to leave Galveston, they just left their sixteen-year-old, Mildred May Knipps, married to Jody Maurice Brooks.

They just left her.

The family quietly speculates what would make Nani leave her daughter like that…apparently leaving her was the only thing to do? Yes, I have a lot of questions, some pity for my grandparents, and more questions we will never know the answers to. They are the kind of questions that begin with, "Are you crazy?! What's wrong with you parents?!"

Nevertheless, the Jody Maurice (Reece) and Mildred Brooks family began and the world began to spin out of control for these two married teenagers.

Deanna Lee Brooks was born in 1937, named after a singer, Deanna Durbin. She weighed more than ten pounds and her father called her "Biggun." and "Dena"

Lena Marie Brooks ("Lin") was born in 1938.

Sandra Maurine ("Sangie Pie") was born in 1939.

Jimmie Lou Brooks ("Jim") came along in 1941.

David Morris Brooks ("Kingfisher" or "King David") was born last in 1943.

I don't know of any nicknames given to the kids by Grandmother, but Grandaddy had plenty of them.

The Brooks home filled up very quickly with children, five of them.

This seems to be where the happiness ended for this marriage, this couple. I know that my grandfather reveled in each child born and longed for more; even if it proved to be physically dangerous for his wife. He delighted in each one, laughed, played and deeply loved each child. Oh how he loved them! And he might have loved his wife for giving them to him if she had let him, if she had just softened a little bit. Would he have? I guess that's a question for the dead who can't answer.

Jody Brooks with Deanna and Lena, Galveston, TX

Chapter 11

Galveston

In April of 2018, I flew to Houston to actually visit Houston and Galveston myself as an adult. Aunt Sandy met me and we stayed at a hotel. I asked which hotel she liked and she said that any of them in a particular chain would do. So I arrived at the hotel in a complex of nice and nicer hotels overshadowed by a billboard that said, SYPHILLIS IS SERIOUS! I hope our hotel is going to be ok. It was, but I had to laugh at the placement of such a sign.

The first day we headed out to Galveston, where it all began, breezy salt air blew gently on a perfect spring afternoon. We wandered through the neighborhoods, mindful of warnings that my mother's first childhood home was not in the best part of town now. It looked fine to us, but we didn't dare knock on the door. We looked at the houses while Aunt Sandy chattered beautiful memories.

A big man opened the front door and stepped out, just to show us that indeed his house was not abandoned. We had been taking pictures of his house and the empty lot beside it where my great-grandmother (Mama Brooks) used to live. Aunt Sandy delightedly told me of the house and how Mama Brooks lived there with my great-grandfather.

Aunt Lena says, "Mama Brooks was the loving member of our family, as well as an adventurer! All of her work history, working on a fish canning row, cooking on a train for the hard-working men. She took several of us out to see where she worked and lived in the Caboose. Huge pots of food steaming on the stove and the best iced tea and desserts… She was well read and you couldn't put anything past her."

Mama Brooks was a force to be reckoned with. She married. After having two children, one of whom was my grandfather, Mama Brooks divorced him and married his brother… for spite.

Marriage is a mighty weapon in my family.

Divorce or no divorce, Mama Brooks offered stability in what I am gathering was a lively and raucous family.

Mama Brooks' second marriage, the one for spite, produced Bayne Brooks. Bayne frightened Aunt Sandy. He used to chase her around with a butcher knife, for fun. This same Bayne Brooks married a woman who also divorced him. She remarried but still wasn't happy. She told her second husband that she still loved Bayne. The second husband then killed her and himself. Aunt Sandy remembers the paperboy selling papers using the headline: "He killed her because he loved her."

I asked Uncle David about Bayne. He said, "He was a homicidal maniac!" After getting into a fight one evening, and being left for dead, he got back up and went into town and killed the man who had beaten him. He continually picked bar fights with the toughest guy at the bar.

Sounds like good reason to give Bayne a wide berth. Still Bayne's name comes up in those memories my mother jotted down. Like her father, he was a pillar in her little life, a pillar with a little dog named Foxxie. Funny how pillars are built playing a steel guitar, yodeling under the pine trees and jumping waves.

Momma wrote:

> In Galveston it was the dark green shutters on the white houses, and lace curtains that covered most windows around those early years from 1937-1945. And those crocheted ring pulls... that dangled from shades...Then the visits to the beach...the sandy paths that I kicked sand - sometimes onto the low stoops of cottages along the beach.

Washday in Mama Brooks' was especially fun. She washed in the upstairs bathroom. Momma said, "I was too little to be leaning out the windows by myself, but I remember seeing her put clothes on a pulley line which she had attached to the chinaberry tree by the garage and pulled in dry and stiff. I could see so many things so high above..."

In one of Momma's journals, she thanked God for Mama Brooks' love. Mama Brooks was certainly the glue that held the family together.

Momma's writing continued:

> At Mama Brooks' I remember admiring a wardrobe with mirrors on the doors and drawers on one side...
>
> A rock garden full of zinnias...

Crawling under the houses, running through the house sitting on the porch bannisters that were wide enough to use as seats... oleander bushes and the smell of wisteria.

There was my great-Granddaddy Jody Edgar Brooks whom we rarely heard about. Little Dena, (Momma) went "honky-tonk-ing" with him. They took walks together. He drank a beer and Dena had an Orange Crush.

> Mother May I, Hopscotch, drawing lines, the skill of not stepping on the lines, spinning around in circles until I fell down, singing, riding "bicycle feet" to feet in bed...
>
> The services at the door: the icemen, milkman who delivered pasteurized milk with cream on the top and in glass bottles...
>
> Taking baths with my sisters, sliding down the back of the white porcelain tub on legs...wild laughter in a tub...playing in boxes with Lena... Lena and me eating butter sugar sandwiches...
>
> I remember Mother chasing Lena around the garage, Lena clinging to a willowy tree and shaking it hard. Lena throwing shingles at our neighbors in our yard from the garage. Lena and me fighting over a doll. Picking lantana bouquets.

The memories often start out "Lena and me..."

> Tall trees, watching the stars from the front porch with Daddy while everyone else was on the lawn...
>
> The icebox was where Daddy put his shaving gear and shaved with a mirror over the icebox.
>
> Steam from the train wheels as we climbed the steps into the train to Galveston. Cracked dark green leather seats and open windows...

The Galveston stories I have heard are the stories of a little girl running free in the summers between her house and her grandmother's. It was childhood bliss with the security of family.

My grandmother had a different take on the time in Galveston:

> We barely made it, having one child after another... I had very little time for myself due to our not having the better things in life (material that is). We had no refrigerator, no washer or dryer (heaven forbid!) - only a sewing machine (treadle type) and a small radio. It took an entire day to feed, clothe, wash by hand on a rub board, hanging out the clothes, ironing at least once a week, cooking and trying to keep our children happy.

In 1942, they moved from Galveston to Houston, Texas, where Uncle David was born. Grandaddy's father came to live with them and died of cancer.

I am not sure when the infidelity occurred or even how it could occur with five little ones around, but my Momma remembers the confrontation.

My snarky self wants to say that Grandmother's infidelity brought their marriage to a screeching halt, but infidelity usually comes long after the marriage is already broken.

She told her children later that she slept with their father's cousin for a one-night stand and it was the best night ever because their dad was always getting her pregnant and she didn't want to be pregnant. No wonder they thought they were not wanted. That was the beginning of their abandonment.

Mildred and Jody Brooks 1945

Chapter 12

June 15, 1945

Grandmother wrote "June 15, 1945... Mr. Brooks and I decided to place our children in the care of Faith Home."

Grandaddy stayed home and slept since he had worked all night. My grandmother took all five of the children to DePelchin Faith Home and left them.

If I allowed my aunts and uncle to fill this page with what they think about that day, that decision, it would be covered in curses washed off by oceans of tears. If this page were a mile square it would not be big enough to contain the sorrow that those words caused five precious children.

Grandmother couldn't have known that her children would remember that day as the day their lives came to an end. It is marked as the most dreadful day of their lives, the day they were left at DePelchin Faith Home.

The summer days of running barefoot over to Grandmother Brooks' house or climbing trees and then coming home again to an intact family were over. The days of knowing Mom and Dad were sleeping in the room next to them were over.

Notes regarding the children's internment with Faith Home showed that my young grandparents were not just young but extremely immature. I wonder if they had known what each of these kids would experience and how it would distort their very souls, would it have made any difference? If they had known that their children would be beaten and suffer many abuses at the hands of caregivers, would they have changed their minds? Would it have made any difference? If they had known that their decisions would mark generations to come, would they have done anything differently?

It seems like my grandparents couldn't have known anything but their own pain. It is easy for me to judge and say what they should have done. I didn't know their poverty or their struggles. I have no way of knowing it.

I do know that the effects of that simple act of leaving five children at DePelchin Faith Home not only injured their souls with lifelong disabilities that seventy-six years later lie about a quarter inch beneath the surface but also left each of them completely unprotected from unnecessary evil. By entrusting that important responsibility to strangers, my grandparents left them unprotected, and unnecessarily vulnerable.

The injuries have never completely healed in any of them, but still fester as a sore that never plans to release them entirely. Yes, they function in amazing ways, but it is still there. Their mother left them and as far as anyone knows showed no remorse for the heinous deed; she only offered excuses of the worst kind that shifted the blame onto five precious children who she said were entirely "ungrateful."

Ungrateful?! I'll say the words. So the children should be grateful that she left them? The children should be grateful that she criticized them at every visit and cried in self-pity? The children should be grateful that they were passed from foster home to Faith Home to foster home and then into the least hospitable and least loving home in Texas, with their own mother? They remain truly grateful for Pine Tree Camp, the special treats of living in an orphanage like a visit from Roy Rogers , and grateful in hindsight for less time with such a mother. I don't think any reasonable person could utter the word grateful and insist that these children swallow it.

Aunt Jennifer (Jimmie Lou) says, "But I still wanted her."

Jody and Mildred Brooks family

Chapter 13

Compassion

I wrote the word "wicked" regarding what my grandparents did and erased it, because Uncle David stopped me. He reminded me that the 1940s were a different time and often there were just no options.

"It was just after the Depression. A lot of people were doing this. Poverty. That's where their mindset was. Not to be on the street. I think we should give something to the parents for doing that to us. Many things were happening."

Maybe they didn't have many options, so much so that even the family couldn't even feed the children. So where was the rest of that big old Texas family? Uncle David reminded me that no one was doing fine back then. Everyone was scrambling to feed their families. Everyone.

Soup kitchens and food lines were a normal part of that time. Malnutrition and death by starvation were not learned in textbooks but by personal experience. Orphans, lots of them, were on the streets. The kids were aware that going to Faith Home was a better alternative than that.

My angry words ring on the page of the injustices inflicted on innocent ones. Innocent. My incensed flaming fury is seventy-six years too late. Apparently 1945 was not the year when outrage was in style. If there was any outrage, it was dismissed or even directed back onto the innocent children.

I imagine the children being ushered into a play area while their mother had a meeting, baby Uncle David perhaps being carried. Some signatures and instructions and my Grandmother left. Did the staff play with the kids, thinking, "I'm glad I'll be gone this evening when the kids figure this out"?

Bright five-year-old Aunt Sandy figured it out the next morning and made her way across the entire campus and back to the office where her mother must surely be waiting, worried sick about her. No, she wasn't there.

Did they hold crying baby Uncle David, kissing his cheeks, shushing him?

Uncle David, I'm having a hard time with that compassion thing. Oh, Uncle David! You stopped me mid rage. I guess you have seen plenty, enough for more than a lifetime, but your comment, "A lot of people were doing this" keeps ringing in my ears. Shamefully, that was David's world, but not David's shame!

The old parable of the blind men and the elephant comes to mind:

> A group of blind men heard that a strange animal, called an elephant, had been brought to the town, but none of them were aware of its shape and form. Out of curiosity, they said, "We must inspect and know it by touch, of which we are capable," So, they sought it out, and when they found it they groped about it. The first person, whose hand landed on the trunk, said, "This being is like a thick snake." For

another one whose hand reached its ear, it seemed like a kind of fan. Another person, whose hand was upon its leg, said, "The elephant is a pillar like a tree-trunk." The blind man who placed his hand upon its side said "The elephant, is a wall." Another who felt its tail, described it as a rope. The last felt its tusk, stating "The elephant is that which is hard, smooth and like a spear."

Perhaps all Uncle David saw was that "a lot of people were doing this."

Perhaps all I have seen is that, "No one in their right mind would do this."

It's a big elephant, this world we live in. Uncle David lived near the hind quarters.

Chapter 14

The Baby Who Cried All the Time

Each child has a different story to tell. Momma, Aunt Lena, and Aunt Sandy remember certain things. Aunt Jennifer has fewer of those memories. Uncle David has no memory of the day he was left at DePelchin Faith Home. He was placed in Wolfe Home (a part of DePelchin Faith Home), a place for the littlest ones, along with Jimmie Lou who changed her name to Jennifer as an adult.

Aunt Jennifer was four years old. Her earliest memories are of a baby crying and crying and the saloon-style swinging doors on the dining hall at Wolfe Home. She isn't sure if the doors were really swinging doors but that is what she remembers. As for the baby crying and crying, she learned later that it was her brother David. It must have tormented her helpless little soul. So strong is the memory of the baby crying that Aunt Jennifer was bothered by crying babies for a long time until someone reminded her that she is now an adult and can do something about a baby crying. How freeing! How imprisoned a child must be to take such emotional baggage so far into adulthood!

Aunt Jennifer says, "David had a box of things that they took away from him so he wouldn't be so upset." (This is the place where

I curse the wisdom of the adults in David's life). It also hurt Aunt Jennifer to watch and know that her little brother was being hurt. According to caseworker notes, Uncle David said, "Mummy is lost."

David Morris Brooks, born in 1942 entered Wolfe Home in 1945, but was put into foster care fairly quickly. He lived with a family who wanted to adopt him. My grandparents would never allow it. The foster family was not keen on raising a boy who would just go back to his biological family. As a foster parent I understand how hard that is. It's messy.

Uncle David had many nice clothes but they were taken away from him because his next stop was the farm. Farm life, good hard work… it sounds good but the reality was quite different. He was one of six boys used as labor on the farm. He was a four year old slave on a farm owned by Annie and George Hilton. Conrad Hilton is a famous name connected with hotels across the world now. Annie and George Hilton were Conrad's aunt and uncle, but their farm was no luxury hotel.

Uncle David says:

> Hard as nails Germans. One of my foster brothers, Don… reminds me that we were beaten regularly for inconsequential things.
>
> I spent 1946-1955 on the farm, Don remembers it as the "Plantation." There were six boys on that farm. We were there to do the work of a working farm. Milk cows (four in the morning, five at night) feed chickens, turkeys (thousands of birds), pigs, cattle. We walked a mile to the school bus stop to get on and off the bus each day. When we got home each day, we would remove our school clothes, get into overalls, do the chores, come in and eat, then do our homework.

Uncle David learned to work hard as a boy slave to hateful, merciless creatures who apparently made very good appearances when the caseworkers came around. He built and fixed fences, split wood. He had to carry a five-gallon bucket of water out to the fence to soften the hard clay ground enough to take the post out.

> There was no running water to the house until 1950, when we got cold running water to a faucet in the sink where a pump was previously. Also we got a butane tank to use for heat instead of the wood stove, and to run our new gas refrigerator. Faith Home gave us a seventeen inch television; the crystal set radio went by the wayside, and we got an electric radio. We had an outhouse at the time I was there. No hot water. We boiled water in big pots poured it into number 3 washtubs, and all bathed in the same water.

When Uncle David speaks of the farm chores, there is a familiarity to me in the list. My Daddy grew up on a farm and worked hard doing many of the same things. His family got the luxury of electricity, bathrooms, etc., at about the same time that the Hiltons did. There is a distinct difference in doing hard work as a slave and doing hard work as a son. Hard work when there is love and family at home is good for a boy.

Where there is no love...well, it changes a boy.

Like Momma, I'm not sure how he turned out so kind and soft toward me when he had so little love when he needed it most.

The Hiltons' grown children came for Sunday dinner. The six foster boys waited hungrily until the Hiltons finished their plates and they were allowed to eat the scraps from the dirty plates. David's sisters remember them being gruff, gambling men. When Momma and her sisters came to visit Uncle David they never visited inside the house.

Momma, Aunt Lena, Aunt Sandy, and Aunt Jennifer visited Uncle David out at the farm. Those four girls were a force, a loud giggling force, dancing and singing their way to the farm. I can see them tumbling out of the car, happy to be together and even happier to see David. David says he has great memories when they came and ugly ones when they left.

"They would get in the car and close the gate, and they drove down the mile-long shell-paved road." They waved all the way while Uncle David sat on a fence watching. "Every time they left, it was ripping us away from any semblance of family." Aunt Sandy says one of her saddest memories is leaving Uncle David at the Hiltons.

Uncle David said that within four years on the farm, he was the oldest and therefore the one responsible to do the work if the others didn't. The last two years at the Hilton farm, Mr. Hilton was in a wheelchair after a car wreck. As a true abuser, he still ruled with an iron fist. Uncle David said, "He would get us trembling saying, 'I'll whoop you, you little pup.' " Even from a wheelchair he could make them tremble.

The saddest part for me is that although Uncle David complained to his caseworkers about the brutality of the Hilton farm, they never listened to him. Shortly after he left the farm to join his mom and sisters in 1955, the other foster boys also left. Uncle David suggests that perhaps there were other complaints and the caseworkers were finally listening to the boys.

Uncle David graciously or perhaps courageously let me read the caseworkers' notes from 1945-1955. There was an obvious disconnect between what Uncle David remembered and what the caseworkers recorded. I saw no record of reports of abuse. They dismissed them. "…A relaxed easy going people who live on a farm" stuck out the pages of the caseworkers' notes. They chalked up Uncle David's discontentment to stubbornness about a particular chore.

Uncle David saw his father about every two years, but an allowance came every month. Uncle David was the only one among his foster brothers who ever had any money. They would go to the little store and David would buy everyone Grapette soda. Yes, of course he did! Mr. Hilton couldn't "tremble" out Uncle David's generous spirit.

Lena, David and Deanna 1954

Jimmie Lou and David 1951

Chapter 15

We Ran Away

While Uncle David was in foster care at the Hilton Farm, the girls were getting accustomed to life at DePelchin Faith Home. They hated it there.

Aunt Lena scaled every tree at Faith Home. She terrified her sisters. Maybe she could find a way to fly away. It certainly was better than fighting their way out. They devised a plan, or perhaps several plans, to escape. Only one materialized.

They left Faith Home just after supper one summer day. That was their outside play time when no one was watching them closely. Through a hole in the fence under the honeysuckle they escaped. Aunt Sandy says, "I remember how exciting it was to be getting away from Faith Home!"

They arrived at Uncle Stanley and Aunt Winnie Mae Sanford's house. Aunt Jennifer says, "I was very surprised that Aunt Winnie Mae just called Faith Home to come and get us. Though in retrospect what could she do with more kids?"

This doesn't really answer any of my questions about where the rest of the family was and why someone couldn't take them. There must have been more but I doubt we will ever know what reason there was for no other family taking the children during the entire ten years they were in Faith Home. Poverty? Perhaps. Or it was it just complicated? Something was terribly wrong.

Some of the caseworkers note that family members tried to take the kids out but there was not much regularity about it. One relative must have been asked about taking some of the kids out to live with her, but she realistically said she couldn't possibly handle the kids. I am sure that if I were there, I would have had to bow out as well. Energetic, traumatized kids - five of them - sounds like a nightmare to me.

Running away turned into a habit for Aunt Sandy. She often ran away not really knowing why she had bolted or what had happened while she was gone. It was frightening to everyone around her. "I realize all the running away was not the fault of anyone but myself. I was such a mixed-up girl… searching for something…perhaps trying to find my way home again to that home I loved and remembered a long time ago. I know now that my Home is with the Lord. In spite of my loneliness or any other problem I have, I always come back to Him and find my rest…eventually. *'For my father and mother have forsaken me but the Lord will take me in.'* Psalm 27:10."

We marvel about that little habit now, as no one can imagine Aunt Sandy running away in such a reckless way. Unimaginable! Her children are most grateful that she didn't bolt when things got hard for their family. It must have taken courage no one could have known about for her to stay, digging in her heels to not give in to abandoning her own children. Even in the midst of chaos Aunt Sandy's children always knew they were wanted and loved.

The cycle of abandonment stopped there.

Chapter 16

Miss McCombs

Someone gave my middle-aged Momma an apple doll. It was the craft of the month for someone. The apple was dried and peeled in such a way to resemble an old woman's face with a little gray wig on top. Two black beads were pushed in for eyes. The wrinkles formed a harsh old woman's face. A high-collared dress and stick arms finished the picture of a stoic old woman pursing her lips.

The doll sat in the foyer of our house on a gold table mounted to the wall. I never understood why she kept it because it was ugly to me and kinda creepy not to mention it being an apple. Momma used to look at the doll and tell me about Miss McCombs, the woman who raised her at Faith Home. I often wonder if some of Momma's propriety had more to do with Miss McCombs than her own family.

Momma said in one of her journals:

> Have thought again of Miss McCombs, puttering around the cottage trying to make it cheerful looking. Remember the colorful dried peppers hanging on the door inside the yellow interior of the closet. She really was attractive and clean looking. It was a sight to see her. Her salt and pepper hair in braids or twist of some sort. For regular days it was

braided and in a knot on the back of her head. Sometimes bangs were formed for a not so severe look, but then she wore a pompadour on the front at first much like the 40's and certainly like the turn of the century. Born around 1884, her breast hung soft and long down her chest and waist and hips were trim. I think her calves were thickest, and though not fat, her ankles were not thin. 6 or 7 shoe. It must be a lot of Irish if she claimed any. Believe she said she was Scottish. Jesse Higgins McCombs. Her eyes were sparkling dark brown if brown. Pale skin which she shaded from the sun with dainty parasols or regular umbrellas. Almost a Roman nose, not hooked, rather haughty look. She didn't have good teeth, a lot of work on them and bridgework, I believe gold teeth filling. Still her teeth were straight.

In the forties people dressed more. She wore gabardine a lot, even stockings and 2-inch heels. I wonder how I could have appreciated her appearance and failed to see herself. She had a sense of humor but it was mean at times to those who misbehaved.

Heaven help us. We spend so much time on frivolous things. Still it is important to remember some things.

It is reassuring to know she, Miss McCombs, was there. Even if she whistled [a reference to the old Irish superstition that a whistling woman and a crowing hen bring bad luck] and swept dirt on Cornelia's [the woman who mopped and waxed the floors] heels as she caught dirt in the cracks that Cornelia missed.

Aunt Sandy remembers the only thing that made Miss McCombs happy was her zinnias. Aunt Sandy can't see Miss McCombs in the same positive light Momma could. In fact all three sisters agree that Momma was probably in denial about exactly how terrible Miss

McCombs was. Aunt Sandy kind of shivers to think about her. Aunt Jennifer calls her "a tall, skinny, old crone." Aunt Lena says, "She was not good or kind at all."

Miss McCombs was not a remarkably happy person. She was also a heartless, abusive disciplinarian. She carried her switch which she called her "keen cutter." She whipped Aunt Jennifer until her legs bled. Seventy-six years later Aunt Sandy and Aunt Jennifer can tell the story about how Miss McCombs flip-flopped down the hall one Sunday morning in her slippers looking for someone to switch. I asked if it was just on Sunday mornings. In unison they both said, "No, just any time she felt the need to switch someone!"

Momma used to use a switch on us, but she was not very motivated to "switch" us into shape. We were sent to cut our switch from the willow tree. Momma did get very mad at times but by the time we came inside, she had lost her steam. We got one little sting. She preferred to let us run all over her.

We did run all over her, but her softness was more powerful than the switch. I need to remember that with my own children. Her softness saved us from a repeat of her childhood. She knew that.

Aunt Sandy says:

> I wet the bed when I was in Miss McCombs cottage but had to sleep in the wet sheets because I was afraid to awaken her. Once Miss McCombs asked the older girls to get me up. They dragged me by my hair down the hall to the bathroom and then hit me on the head crowning me 'Queen Sandra'. I told Miss McCombs and that never happened again.

No one would want to live with Miss McCombs, but she provided much-needed stability. She demanded order. You would be okay if you could stay away from her "keen cutter."

The only one worse than Miss McCombs at Faith Home was the substitute cottage mother, Miss Gentry, who came once a month for a few days. My aunts haven't expounded much on the things she did, but each of the sisters have ugly memories of her. They did share that Miss Gentry spent her days doling out humiliating discipline, taping the children's mouths closed when they talked too much while sitting in their panties against the wall waiting for showers. She then inspected their washing and threw them back into the shower if it wasn't done properly.

I remember bathing my own children. The bathroom floor got wet. I got wet. Sometimes I was not patient when they splashed me. Curse those rubber toys that shoot water! My husband and I chased naked babies who escaped the towel giggling, grabbing them and wrapping them in laughing hugs. We diapered, pajamaed, and kissed clean cheeks.

There was no time for hugging or kissing clean cheeks in my mother's childhood universe, but she gave that to me, and I have given it to my children.

How did she know how to give us that?!

I am grateful.

Chapter 17

Little Girl in the Bathtub

Not knowing much about Little Girl's past, I approached bath time with concern that I not traumatize her. Door wide open. The guys were instructed to steer clear. We filled the tub. It was in the tub that I learned how severely she lacked language skills. She had not been taught parts of the body or how to count her precious toes. She did know how to giggle. And she giggled a lot as we bubble bathed, bath bombed and scrubbed her beautiful dark skin with my translucent white (almost old) hands. Older and wiser, I did not buy squirt toys this time around, but foam letters which ended up as clothing on one of her Barbie dolls. The letter "O" made a nice miniskirt.

After a few weeks, I thought that I should probably teach Little Girl to bathe herself since I expected my kids to bathe themselves at this age. Her brown eyes had a look of doubt in them. Was I going to leave her? So I asked what was wrong. She said,"Well, my mom never really gave me a bath and she usually sent me to give baths to the other kids. I don't really know how."

My heart felt the pain hers should have registered, but she was past measuring pain. It was just her life and I was the one who thought a mom ought to give her little girl a bath. As she said,"It's very different in my house." So I suggested that since her mom never bathed her that I would keep on bathing her, just for fun. She should just pay attention about how to do it so that she could take care of her baths when she went back home.

"Back home": the day we hoped would never come. Would it be enough that she would know how to take a bath by herself? And oh what funny bath chats we had while she soaked and I folded laundry right beside her until her hands reached just the right wrinkly state.

My grandmother missed a lot.

Chapter 18

Life at DePelchin Faith Home

Life at DePelchin Faith Home in the beginning was all difficult. Five children became accustomed to a life of trauma and anxiety. Anger, aggression, withdrawal, crying, lots of crying, bedwetting, stubbornness, resistance to any structure placed around them… all of this marked every minute of their existence in institutional living.

Aunt Sandy (five years old) would not comb her hair or pay any attention to her appearance. She wouldn't eat. She refused to acknowledge any conversation that didn't get her back to her intact family on Melwood Street. They said Momma (eight years old) wasn't as damaged by everything because she withdrew. She was imploding. Uncle David (two years old) just cried…a lot. I am not sure how the garden walls of DePelchin Faith Home could contain such sadness and despair.

The children, each in their own way, became accustomed to the people who cared about their life, albeit paid and temporary kinds of people. The walk to the caseworkers' office became a regular route as they discussed accepting the new reality that included betrayal by their parents (although it was never called that). It was just the beginning of the lifelong journey through accepting what they never should have to accept. Caseworkers called them stubborn and disturbed. Someone disturbed them for sure and that stubbornness? Well, they could all own that.

School work started falling into place and the kids all stayed on grade level although not making the kind of grades that showed their intelligence. In foster care that is called success. Sometimes foster kids are three or four years behind so DePelchin Faith Home accomplished what was most certainly in the range of "extremely successful" childcare.

There was so much bedwetting! It appears in notes as the kids were so concerned about it. I can't even imagine the piles of laundry created just by the Brooks children. They were given access to psychiatric care. It's hard to say what went on in those clinical visits, but someone was trying and offering help.

Momma, Aunt Lena, and Aunt Sandra were in Miss McCombs' cottage. They hated her because she switched them for wetting the bed among other infractions. Then there were other girls and cruelty that comes from housing a whole bunch of "disturbed" children together and expecting them to get along in angelic ways. It just doesn't happen. One girl was singled out as influencing two of the sisters to skip school on two different occasions. Momma watched over Aunt Jennifer when she felt like she was being pulled into a bad crowd.

I wish I could right the wrong of five innocent children being abandoned and abused over and over again. Of course that is impossible and even saying it was wrong doesn't really fix anything. Perhaps it does set some of the untold story straight. Perhaps. Each of these children, now the most lovely senior citizens you could ever know, have at different times had their moments when they felt the truth must be shouted, but mostly they want the truth of the extraordinary childhood they were tossed into remembered for its remarkable moments.

It's not that they never had any fun at Faith Home. We always heard about the dancing.

I can't really imagine talking about Faith Home without mentioning the dancing. There were dances even in harsh Mrs. McCombs' cottage in the living room. Momma was one of the older girls who jitterbugged and swing danced. There were also dances in

Mrs. Brockway's cottage. Music and dancing didn't solve everything, but what a fun distraction!

Years later Momma always cut a few moves in the kitchen. She used to dance down the grocery store aisles with her arms over me pushing the cart as we went, clicking her heels in the air. I loved it until I got old enough to realize that we were dancing in a grocery store and my mother was clicking her heels… in a grocery store! She brushed off my embarrassment and did a little extra to her routine, just for fun. DePelchin Faith Home gave us the joy (or embarrassment) of watching Momma dance.

And then there was the "rec hall." Events such as square dances, called by a man named Cricket, happened there. It was known as a happy place on the campus of Faith Home. Roy Rogers came with his horse Trigger, right inside the rec hall! Who gets to see Roy Rogers and Trigger? DePelchin Faith Home kids did! Aunt Jennifer still swoons, "He shook my hand and I didn't want to wash it." Gene Autry, tipsy enough to fall off of his horse, also made an appearance.

Faith Home, albeit sometimes harsh and difficult, provided stability that enabled the children to do many things that a completely dysfunctional home would never have allowed. Momma was able to excel as a synchronized swimmer, performing with the high school team at the iconic and glamorous Houston Riviera, the Shamrock Hotel. The kids were exposed to many forms of education that poverty would have never allowed.

The girls all had either piano or dance lessons. Momma had piano lessons for about three years. One of my favorite memories as a child was when Momma played the piano. My sister and I twirled into the curtains and waltzed to whatever she played. It was just enough to give me the insatiable urge to play the piano and my sister the insatiable urge to dance. Very quickly Momma would move over and let me take over the piano for hours. My favorite was to play something that would bring Momma to my side with happy tears. I always give my parents credit for sacrificing for my piano lessons. Even when Daddy was unemployed for periods of time I never missed a lesson in ten years. Momma taught me the joy in music. DePelchin enabled me to learn to love the piano. I am grateful.

Dena Brooks

Chapter 19

Cabbages

My friend Ruth Tinsley said this about raising high-spirited children:

"When we would be bemoaning our strong-willed children, my Grandmother Averitt would remind us that we could raise racehorses or we could raise cabbages. Cabbages are much easier to raise, but racehorses are exceedingly more valuable!!"

After reading some of the caseworkers' notes on the Brooks children, I am convinced that those children were indeed racehorses-valuable exotic racehorses that refused to be turned into cabbages. They wouldn't be easily raised in rows. Their legs needed to stretch and pound the course with tails up, stretching forward to win by a nose.

Cabbages would be easier for a children's home.

I often tell discouraged mothers that no one else is better equipped to parent their child than they are. I remember feeling a helpless despair in mothering my first beautiful girl. I could think of several people who would be much better, more consistent. I wasn't capable of the requirements of one child much less the four God sent my way.

Grandmother must have felt the same way and then her marriage failed. My grandparents could have united and raised some fine racehorses but when they couldn't DePelchin Faith Home stepped in. But the Home didn't have the right understanding.

They understood cabbages.

Cabbages! Yes, Faith Home would have been happier with cabbages. Much of the caseworkers' notes centered around getting the children to adjust to institutional living, keeping them in line, preventing them from causing problems, solving bed wetting problems, ridding them of aberrant behavior, sending them to counseling visits, which mostly seemed to be disconnected from the horrifying loss of the family unit. Instead of normal fighting among siblings, their squabbles became an expression of anger and loss, abuse and upheaval with no known tools to deal with the pain coursing through their little bodies. They had no idea what to do with this new universe they had been dropped off into and expected to excel in. They were expected to be good little children not these traumatized kids who desperately just wanted to go back to the little house on Melwood Street where the billboard beside the house was covered with morning glories and the shade trees sheltered them.

Well maybe it wasn't all morning glories. I understand that at least once the neighbor shut all the kids in a chicken coop and called their mother to come get them. Of course they were trouble before they got to Faith Home. All children are trouble.

I have four kids who made sure through their behavior that my motherly pride was nicely packed away and not on display too often. One of our children was fondly known as *el terremoto chico* or "the little earthquake." Everywhere that child went, the earth moved, sometimes quite literally. Our neighbor, was also familiar with the antics, but she was a wise woman. She recognized that such behavior was part of the making of a fine human being.

As a pastor's wife, I quickly let go of the fantasy that my kids would be the perfect ones. I think it was probably the first week of our daughter's life when I realized that controlling another person, however small they may be, can be done, but the cost is too high. Of course, controlling the child that took his clothes off outside the front door of the church on a Sunday morning might have been a good idea, but children are squirrelly and sometimes, or perhaps most of the time, they get the best of us, slipping by and getting into trouble. Despite the mischief, that child is one of my favorite people in the whole world and I love listening to his thoughts. I love seeing the people my squirrelly children have become and are becoming and am so grateful that my neighbors did not have a chicken coop.

Chapter 20

The Blessing of Faith Home

Little Girl was our first foster child. We hadn't a clue what we were getting into. We had no idea how much we would love her and grieve her absence when she went back to her family. We weren't the first family she had gone to. When I got one of those calls, "Six-year-old Hispanic girl… can you take her?" I said "Yes. But I need a couple of days." I don't even remember what the delays were that kept me from taking her immediately. As her language abilities progressed she was able to tell me about the places she went before she came to us… my heart broke. I let her go some other place for two whole days! What kind of a mother am I and why did I think anything was more important than this precious little girl?! It could have been a bad place. We know about bad places now.

DePelchin Faith Home would have been an excellent home for children if it weren't for that thing called "abandonment" and the disfiguring blow to a child's psyche. The abandonment took precedence in every part of the Brooks children's brains.

Faith Home was a good place, as places go. It was relatively safe. The children were well fed, taught many things that they needed for life.

When Momma talked about the tile floors, all shiny and polished, and her little cubbyhole where she kept her things, her very own things, she said it was as if they were rich. Employees cooked and cleaned. Their laundry was washed, ironed, mended by someone. They were given privileges few children in all of the United States had. They still hated it there.

Aunt Sandy said that as an adult, "I visited a lady from church who had Alzheimer's. She was heading back to her room and went to the doors, crying to be let out. I had to stop visiting her because it reminded me of being locked in at Faith Home."

It was a lovely prison.

I'm a little old to be just now figuring some things out… things like the fact that having parents gives us freedom and security that can't be found in the largest mansion with highly paid bodyguards. All kids need parents who are loving and somewhat accessible.

Faith Home was a blessing. There were plenty of places kids could end up that weren't safe. The girls knew that, but abandonment colored every inch of their lives.

Chapter 21

About Foster Homes

I felt a wave of nausea when I read the caseworker's description of the Hilton foster home as being run by a simple and relaxed couple who didn't see bad behavior as a deterrent for taking a child. A relaxed, rural environment was indeed just what those kids needed. It disturbs me because we have been pursued as foster parents for precisely the same reasons: rural, relaxed, experienced, older couple. We could have been those Hiltons!

When the caseworkers drove away from the Hilton farm, the hellish nightmare began in a hard, loveless home. Slave labor surrounded innocent little boys. The caseworkers listened to the boys' complaints about harsh beatings only years after the placement. Too late.

Other foster homes were a welcome reprieve from Faith Home but it was always a mixed bag. The Countryman foster home was pure joy for Aunt Sandy. "Mrs. Countryman was a wonderful cook and took great care of us, but she was rather strict. I ran away one time but came back that evening." She loved them.

Foster homes were not pure joy for others. Even the Countryman foster home had big problems.

But foster moms helped the kids quit wetting the bed. I am so glad, because there was a lot of bedwetting and it troubled the kids so much. At least that humiliation came to an end.

The boarding rates were carefully recorded since Grandaddy was paying quite handsomely and shamelessly for someone else to raise his kids. Thirty-five dollars a month per child was the going rate in 1950, less if they lived at Faith Home.

The caseworkers' notes show the girls begging for this and that. As passionately as they had wanted to be in a foster home they then begged to be at Faith Home. One sister influenced another and couldn't get along with this foster parent or that sister. It appears the Brooks girls ran circles around the caseworkers. I kinda feel sorry for them, the caseworkers, that is. The children were not allowed to make the decision about where they stayed but they certainly did work hard at persuasion. There were many "aha" moments after the fact for these caseworkers. One wrote, "Later I understood that Deanna had been instrumental in trying to urge Lena and Sandra to return to Faith Home rather than back to their foster home."

It is very hard to tell when there were legitimate complaints. If there was abuse it certainly was in the middle of the pile of confusion that was the norm for the four Brooks girls. It would have taken a very astute and interested caseworker to really understand what was going on in foster care and at DePelchin Faith Home.

Caseworkers today only last a couple of years at best because the stress level is so high. These caseworkers were no different. We can read how the caseworkers tried very diligently to keep good notes because soon they would no longer be the "go-to" person for the girls. The girls knew it and worked the system as best they could, sometimes for safety, sometimes just because they could.

One of the girls "expressed some fear that when I [the caseworker] left Faith Home that all of this would be forgotten and they would have to remain in their foster home forever and be unhappy."

Two pages of notes later: "This case is being transferred to Mrs. _____."

Really?!

Yet in the midst of the chaos there were moments that the kids treasured as if they are burned into their souls: little memories, big memories, a kindness here or there. Aunt Sandy gathered eggs at her foster home. She remembers Mrs. Countryman teaching her how to hold the hen's head down to get eggs without getting pecked. My hens were not impressed and squawked loudly at the interference when Aunt Sandy gathered eggs from my hens. Aunt Sandy continuing to reminisce about her time with Mrs. Countryman, whispered like a little girl, "And I loved the lambs." So much of what they remember barely fits with the cold caseworkers' chaotic notes about the children's complaints. I hardly know what to believe except that the things the Brooks siblings remember is in every sense real to them and therefore important, more important than the meticulous and sometimes stupid notes taken by caseworkers.

The truth of every foster home, institutional home, or even family home is that it is always a mixed bag. The foster mom group chat I am involved in showed one foster mom's frustration, "So I'm just really sad and wishing I could magically handle things better somehow. Super imaginary foster mom would have waited patiently… but I broke down and yelled." Every mother can relate to the daily failings in caring for our children. Children in foster care have some of these moms caring for them. There is always something negative, something very wrong, something very right.

Somewhere in there we hope that there is enough right to allow a child to grow up as they should.

I myself wonder if the time with our precious Little Girl was enough. We know she went back into trauma and abuse, but we wonder: Will the precious tender year of helping her walk through the trauma in her little life be enough? Did we love her enough? Will she remember or will they beat the memories of us out of her?

According to Dr. Bessel van der Kolk, author of The Body Keeps the Score, "If you carry a memory of having felt safe with somebody long ago, the traces of that earlier affection can be reactivated in attuned relationships when you are an adult." [1]

Oh Dr. Van der Kolk! I am counting on it!

It's a sketchy way to grow up, in an orphanage, foster care, or with parents who can't get it together.

There must have been someone in Momma's life who made her feel safe. That makes it worth it for me to imperfectly love foster children.

---

[1] Bessel van der Kolk M.D., The Body Keeps the Score: Brain, Mind, and Body in the Healing of Trauma. (New York: Penguin Books, 2014).

Chapter 22

Daddy's Home!

My Grandaddy was a presence. You could call him a "swashbuckler". You can just tell by the photos of a man peering through glasses, with his hands on his hips, with a wide happy smile. He was the hero of the story and there were five little children in need of saving. He returned from working abroad every so often. Aunt Jennifer said that when he came to town everyone was happy. He smiled all the time and spoiled the kids rotten. He traveled to exotic places like Guam and Saudi Arabia, bringing back trinkets and pictures.

Aunt Sandy remembers, "We went to the Forum Cafeteria and we got anything we wanted. If we didn't like it we didn't have to eat it. Mother would have been so angry at wasting food."

In sorting through Momma's things I found a tourist book of NY. I didn't want a tourist book of New York, but Aunt Sandy opened it and saw familiar handwriting. She drew her breath in with a gasp. Her Dad had written notes to each child, describing the sights in New York City. It appears that the kids were never far from his mind. Aunt Lena remembers wondering why they couldn't go with him.

I sat beside Uncle David looking at black and white pictures of his father, my grandfather. There is no doubt that the genetic resemblance is there. He has the same stance, the same wide smile. He could be mistaken for his father easily. He didn't get the essentials of manhood from fishing together or working on cars together. I'd like to say he got them from visits, but the visits were so few and far between. It must have been a bit confusing. I find Uncle David a delightful, caring uncle who still figured out what it meant to be a man.

Aunt Sandy said that it was like they were kept in a birdcage and her daddy took them out to play. He was a hero to them. He was capable of anything and everything except marriage and family and taking them away from Faith Home. It appeared his hands were tied. When Aunt Jennifer was hatefully disciplined for a small crime, they all told him, their hero. He couldn't do anything about it because he couldn't take the kids with him.

My granddaddy, Jody Brooks, just wasn't around much. I asked Uncle David in particular about his absentee father. He says, "Uncle Norman was my go-to guy when I needed a bike tire or anything." I met Uncle Norman when he was an old man. He was kind. I can see that easily. There is even evidence that he tried to take Uncle David out of Faith Home and foster care, but the wheels of childcare for a "ward of the state" grind very slowly. There were other uncles and of course the abusive Mr. Hilton who impacted Uncle David's life, but like all the children, they longed for the larger-than-life man, who wrote letters fairly regularly, sent an allowance and was distinctly absent.

Aunt Jennifer says, "I thought he was a nice guy, but only saw him about six times in my life." Grandaddy comforted himself in his absence saying that his children would rather he make a lot of money than be present and unable to buy things for them. He was okay with being a "nice guy."

For a foster kid among orphans, having an absent father was to be envied, but bragging rights and some pocket change were all the kids had.

Miss McCombs confronted Momma on her little private fantasy. "You just think your Daddy is going to come riding in on a white horse and save you. Well, he isn't!"

Aunt Sandy says, "He was a god to me."

Perhaps he was as helpless as they, but he gave them hope.

Aunt Sandy remembers a watershed moment with her father. It had been months since (teenage) Aunt Sandy had seen her father. She had gotten into serious trouble this time when she ran away. Instead of taking her into his arms, he yelled at her for her crime, venting his own frustration on his precious girl. He left. She had a breakdown. They tried to console her, but she could not be consoled. Finally someone took her down to the soda shop and bought her a Coke. Aunt Sandy says,"That Coke tasted so good!" The crying subsided at last.

When she collected herself a judge asked her who she wanted to live with, her mother or her father, she placed the dagger firmly into her father with her answer. "With Mother." After many years in DePelchin Faith Home care, the children had learned enough to know that living with their mother was the worst of the choices available to them. Aunt Sandy said she didn't know what she was thinking because going to live with her Mother was about the most painful decision any of them could think of. Her father ran out of the room. Sandy immediately regretted her words and chased after him into the hallway. The elevator doors closed in her face. That was the last time she ever saw him. Jody Maurice Brooks died a year later.

Grandmother's words regarding his death, " All I could think of is I had to take it all (the children ...taking their unhappiness out on me.) while your dad laid in his grave escaping all this."

Jody Brooks

Jody Brooks, Guam

Chapter 23

Little Girl Perched

Our Little Girl often played with Roger and our son, reveling in being tossed about and flipped upside down, chased and caught. As the days neared for her to return to her family she seemed to want to absorb as much of Roger as possible. She always finished eating first and made her way over to Roger's chair. She climbed him like a tree and perched on his shoulder like a bird. I guess we could have corrected her, but it was too fun watching him try to finish eating, laughing as she made those last few bites nearly impossible. She needed his strength. So she soaked up "Tio" until her little heart was just the right "wrinkly" and we let her do it.

All children need a father of some sort. Boys need a man to teach them how to be a man. A girl needs a father as well. Without him they may grow hungry for perhaps any man. Hungry girls are often abused by men who can sniff out their needs like a bloodhound. That fatherly influence is protection in every way, even when Daddy isn't around. The security of having a father present helps children to grow and mature physically, intellectually and emotionally.

A few years ago I wouldn't have believed that last statement. Really? How can a father's presence help a child grow physically? I believe it now because I have seen it with my own eyes. Little Girl came to us stunted in every way, but (according to her counselor and caseworker) as soon as she felt safe, that child grew and grew and grew. I marked her growth weekly instead of yearly. She had grown an entire inch in one month. Her baby teeth were falling out at an alarming rate and permanent ones were coming in. She grew so much that her own mother maintained a shocked expression during their entire first visit. Little Girl continued to grow and grow in every way, turning into a confident little girl who no one really recognized. She finally felt safe.

Those Brooks kids were already vibrant children, tall and strong. I wonder what they would have looked like if their daddy had stayed around.

That leads me to look at all five with a bit of awe. Asking questions like "How…? How did you turn out so kind, so clever, so successful when the entire world was steamrolling over your poor bodies and minds? How…?"

Silly questions.

I am so proud to be related to such people who survived and even excelled, in spite of or perhaps because of suffering such unbelievable pain.

Chapter 24

Mother

When my own daughter turned eight years old, I looked into her gray blue eyes and wondered how Grandmother could put her precious child, much less children, into some other place, no matter how safe, no matter how much the children needed to be fed and clothed, no matter how deep her poverty... How could she?! My cousin, Donna, confessed to asking the same thing. She felt the same way. We just can't understand.

Even now as a mother, we, her granddaughters, can't get past what Grandmother did to her own children. The level of selfishness is unthinkable. It seems like whatever was the worst decision, that is what Grandmother did, even as an old woman. She left a wake of brokenness behind her.

But she was broken, too.

Everyone really wants to see that Grandmother did something good, but the cutting sarcasm and bitterness shadow anything good.

My aunts say she called them her big fat daughters."

Aunt Jennifer says that Grandmother was old before her time. Yes, she was old and bitter before she was even twenty-five. She was old and bitter with moments of softness.

There were rare occasions when the sweetness they longed for showed up. Aunt Sandy says that one time they were riding with their dad in his car and her mother was on the side of the road with gum to give them. The kids pleaded with their dad, "Slow down! It's Mother!" His anger that had brewed hot during the divorce seemed to power the car. He sped up. Grandmother quickly tossed the gifts into the open window.

Momma said that one time Grandmother had planned a picnic at the movies where everyone got to eat a good portion. It was all she had and she was trying. Aunt Jennifer remembers that little picnic too. It must have been a sweet day.

Those are just bits and pieces of goodness. It was the boulders of constant abandonment and then she tossed pebbles of selfish criticism and blame that these heavy-laden children felt the most.

Aunt Jennifer tried to explain that "…when a mother comes to visit and then leaves for a month it is constant abandonment. She was doing the best she could. I made the mistake of saying something mouthy when I was on a visit with Daddy and he let me know that he didn't like it. Mother took all phrases as an accusation of her. I always wanted my friend's mom. Mother didn't have much self-worth. didn't want to admit it but when she came to Faith Home she would be angry, crying, or critical."

Oh, why did she make her children scrounge for crumbs of love and affection from the very one who should have drenched them in love?! It would have helped everyone for generations if she had just said she was sorry a long time ago.

Grandmother must have thought that uttering the words "I'm sorry" would open the door to what she already felt was overwhelming criticism from her children. I have often thought that she knew quite well the gravity of abandonment and its effect on Momma, Aunt Lena, Aunt Sandy, Aunt Jennifer, and Uncle David. But if she uttered the words, she would have to bear the responsibility of them and that was so much more than her small shoulders could bear. She was indeed a woman to be pitied. Arguing with her was a useless effort. She had calloused that part of her heart so thickly, only God Himself could melt such hardness.

I think all five would have appreciated an apology from Grandmother. At one point it weighed so heavily on Aunt Sandy that she wrote her a direct letter asking for an apology.

2/24/1986 [Aunt Sandy to Momma regarding letter asking for apology]

> Mother has not said one word about what I wrote about. I wrote her back and said I'd like to have a reply of some kind. She wrote back and never said a thing about it again. I'm puzzled. Guess I'll call her sometime when I get brave enough. It really hurts to know she isn't going to say a thing. I feel that she feels it will either blow over and she'll just wait, she can't deal with it or she won't deal with it. I'm thinking that she won't and that hurts the worst. I feel that I should be important enough to get a reply.
>
> If she thinks that I'm just supposed to automatically know that she's sorry, she better think again. Somewhere in all these years, there should have been some mention of that. I've asked her to forgive me for all I've done. Why can't she? I hate that all of a sudden it's become so important but it has.

> Sometimes I feel that if Mother says she's sorry then we won't be the guilty ones any more and she'll have to feel more guilt. It's as if she's holding that over us and can't release her grip.
>
> It seems as if you don't feel the same as I do so maybe I shouldn't say "we." We each have our own separate feelings as we each had a slightly different life.

I never sensed that Momma needed an apology. She didn't ask for one as far as I know. There was a tiny note scribbled in Mom's handwriting that said, "Don't you think she feels guilty?" It seemed she had some empathy for the guilt her mother bore. Probably a more accurate assessment of Momma not needing an apology is that she never thought she deserved one because she was nothing. It wasn't a false or put-on humility.

Momma literally thought she was nothing.

> Well, I got my answer from Mother...
>
> I don't know why this has suddenly become so important to me. In God's eyes we are supposed to confront those in love that we have ought against and talk things over. I wish it could be that way with Mother but I guess she can't do that. My letter was a heart cry from a daughter for the first time in 46 years to her mother - but she sees it as condemning her. I guess I just have this mushy picture of a mother saying "I'm sorry you were so hurt. Please forgive me." But it can never be from Mother.
>
> Nothing she did ever said she was sorry to me because she was always so angry and I never felt that she cared about me. Her anger in the letter even reinforces that even more...

Grandmother would never admit any wrongdoing or say she was sorry; she didn't like to talk about it. When Aunt Sandy pressed the subject she finally said she was going to take Aunt Sandy out of her will if she didn't stop talking about it.

It wasn't the relationship she wanted, but at least she had a relationship with her mother. When Aunt Sandy let the matter go, she prayed, "God, you can have… Mother. If she never gives me the apology I want, that's okay." If she ever did, it would be a gift. She never did and it really was okay. Letting go of her need for an apology was precious freedom for Aunt Sandy.

My thoughts about Grandmother have always been fairly harsh. It's the mother in me judging her, but I would want someone to be kind and gracious to me if I were caught in the midst of my worst parenting moments. I would. I do feel sorry for her. Somehow she was incapable of the love the kids needed. Grandmother just didn't have it to give and Grandaddy didn't have enough to cover her with his love.

I do notice that Grandaddy flew in and wowed the kids. It was an unfair comparison. Grandmother struggled to visit and see the children, but she kept coming. She stayed at it even though her visits were not appreciated and she was generally a mess every time. She kept trying. I guess that counts.

Mildred and Deanna

Mildred

Chapter 25

I Hurt Her

It was just one word, but apparently I had used it before to describe one of my kids and she had been silent then. It was a critical word. So now I used it again and the end of the phone went silent. She didn't pick up when I called back. I had broken her with one word. My heart broke at the senseless pain I had inflicted and there was no backing up and doing it over. She did finally call back and wailed into the phone, spewing anger at me. And I couldn't say "I'm sorry" enough. She wasn't looking for "I'm sorry." I don't even know what she was looking for but whatever it was, I couldn't provide it.

The same evening a friend called. Funny that she had received a call from her adult child, raging into her ear all the anger of her childhood. I had nothing but tears for my friend. Nothing.

Several of the Brooks siblings had similar conversations with their mother. They raged about the abandonment, asking questions. She answered with blame shifting, finally shutting each one down succinctly. Grandmother couldn't go there with her kids. I can hardly go there with mine.

I had a very different mother. She was soft and loving. She wasn't perfect and there were horrible moments. Horrible. But her children love her. Everyone loved her. Everyone overlooked the horrible.

I hope mine will overlook my "horrible."

Chapter 26

Electric and Extraordinary!

The photo albums contain photos of Momma, Aunt Lena, Aunt Sandy, and Aunt Jennifer (Jimmie Lou). Sometimes Uncle David was in the photos too. There were more of him as an adult in the navy. They always looked like they were having such a good time or so I thought. To hear Momma's selective memory of Faith Home I had imagined it to be like that old movie, Seven Brides for Seven Brothers, girls dancing in petticoats around the bedposts. I think that it actually was sometimes like that. The kids had a great time singing everywhere they went, laughing, lots of laughing, dancing. The activities kept them moving and not thinking so much about the great losses of what brought each child to Faith Home. It was when the five siblings were together that the oppressive nature of life at Faith Home was forgotten. They lit up like lightbulbs!

Nothing changed as they became adults. My aunts gathered together in Aunt Sandy's home. Laughter exploded in the kitchen. It was not a regular thing so I remember them dancing, cracking eggs with one hand, laughing and jabbing each other. They giggled and sang and we all smiled. There was so much dancing and so much laughter. Then Aunt Lena would let a cuss word fly and Mom and

Aunt Sandy would run to their corners and the moment was over… for a moment…but they couldn't stand to be away from each other. It was impossible to cram a missed childhood together into a weekend, but they tried.

They were and are extraordinary! The vivacious smiles, posing, and the showing of a little leg or perhaps those saddle oxfords, jump out of the photo album.

The family connection is a bit like electricity. It's there and powers the whole house, but you can't see it. These girls had it and sparks flew whenever they were together. It was dangerous sometimes, but they couldn't stay away. Nor can I stay away from them.

The joy of Momma's siblings oozed and spewed, soothing deep wounds if only because they completely understood each other when it came to the suffering. Having someone to understand is rare treasure.

Jimmie Lou, Lena, Sandy, Dena

Dena, Jimmie Lou, Sandy, Lena, David at the Hilton Farm

Jimmie Lou, Lena, Sandy, Dena

Jimmie Lou, Sandy, Lena, Dena

107

Jimmie Lou and Lena

Dena and Lena

Chapter 27

The House at Delafield

As we exited the highway in Houston Aunt Sandy said excitedly, "Let me show you the house at Delafield!" I think I was supposed to know what the "house at Delafield" was, but Momma had never explained it to me. Sandy pulled up in front of an old light green house in an older neighborhood while she talked about it. It has taken me a while to understand that the house at Delafield was not so much an address as it was a symbol of freedom, precious freedom. The kids had been held captive in their various prisons: Faith Home, foster homes, or for David, the slave labor of the Hilton farm. They were free at last! Ten years after being left at Depelchin Faith Home their daddy had rented a house. He hired their mother as housekeeper, and they were to all live together, (all except Daddy who was working out of the country.)

The house at Delafield held different joys for each child. Aunt Jennifer remembers a cat named "Didhebitecha." For 14-year-year-old Uncle David the house at Delafield meant a bike and no supervision. What could possibly go wrong?! He roamed the neighborhood, apparently with a big smile on his face. He smiles about it even now. He lived for the first time in his memory with his mother and four older sisters.

Uncle David remembers that the greatest loss in living at the Hilton farm was the loss of family. "I didn't really know my sisters, Dena least of all. She was an Esther Williams synchronized swimmer, a really big deal! Never saw her synchronized swimming, but when she lived in Charlotte, we raced in a public pool. She kicked my butt. I thought I could swim fast."

After watching them drive away over and over again, this time they all got to stay together!

Apparently it was the summer of all summers which included knocking out the street light so it didn't shine in Uncle David's window at night. His "resort vacation" at Delafield continued for three years, but Grandmother couldn't last that long. She couldn't be without a man very long. In just a few months she met a man at a dance and ran off to marry her third husband. He was a tall, dark, handsome, striking, sociopath who nearly killed her in a jealous rage when she got up one night to go to the bathroom. Mr. King put a hole in her jaw and damaged her vocal cords. Her face looked like someone in a war zone and her voice was never the same after that. She left to heal in El Paso with her mother, Nani, and stayed there. The kids were left alone for three days.

The place that was supposed to make up for ten years of institutional care became the next place of abandonment and horrific trauma. That's a lot of unrealistic expectations for a house and a single mother. Once again, Grandmother had the opportunity to love and care for her children, but she proved she couldn't possibly change the pattern of dysfunctional abandonment she had inadvertently practiced on the children all of their lives. She just left them… again.

Momma says:

"Tragedy struck…Mother married."

I would add "again." This marriage was a humdinger! But her marriage wasn't entirely to blame for the disasters that followed. It was simply the last straw.

Mama Brooks showed up to care for them. She stayed until 1958.

Momma and Aunt Lena moved to an apartment.

Aunt Lena says, "Our first apartment was above a carpet company across the street from St. Anne's Catholic Church that I attended and got married in. Dena and I would eat at a little restaurant no bigger than our living room. It was called the Toddle House and it had the best small cottage potatoes covered in paprika ever. Delicious! Neither of us could cook much, so we ate in cheap restaurants in the neighborhood. She made sandwiches for our lunches and I made meatloaf and whatever.

"The second and last apartment was much bigger and better and being two 'beauties' we turned a few heads!"

"Dena was the head secretary to the CEO of Schlumberger Oil Company… with the better pay, she bought some of the most beautiful clothes and I was so happy to see her enjoying having such pretty, extravagant things. She bought me a beautiful ring with a green semi-precious stone in the middle with some tiny diamonds (not real, I'm sure) around it. When I lost it years afterwards, I just cried. She was very generous with her money, and in fact, I was as well. We knew about trying to make people happy by finding just the right gift."

I was so glad to get these comments from Aunt Lena, to know that there had been a bright spot before the siblings dispersed.

Momma's notes say, "Lena married. Dena floundered badly. As she had been." It was so hard that Momma wrote about herself in third person.

All of the children floundered in one way or another. It was an unrealistic expectation to think that living with their mother after all those years would enable the family to be any more cohesive. It was more like the blossom of an ugly invasive weed planted on June 15, 1945. If you throw enough manure on anything it will grow and bloom eventually. They had certainly had the manure and this was the bloom: "tragedy" as Momma called it.

The children would spend a lifetime whacking that weed and its stenchy bloom in therapy, church, and with kind friends.

The House at Delafield

David and his bike

Sandy, Mama Brooks, Dena, and Lena

Chapter 28

Grandmother's Husbands

The caseworkers' notes and letters to and from the parents read like a bad novel that should have a feigned happy ending. This one doesn't exactly have one of those endings. The caseworkers initially referred to my grandparents as Mr. Brooks and then Mrs. Brooks. It didn't take long for Mrs. Brooks to become Mrs. Jolley. I suspect she was looking for her happily ever after too.

Mr. J.C. Jolley, the first man she married after my grandfather, was a widower, thin, not too tall, and he never smiled. He didn't like Aunt Sandy, so he hardly said anything to her. If he cared for Grandmother's children, he didn't show it by coming to visit the kids. He golfed and liked baseball. The five siblings remember his two daughters as "friendly," but the caseworker notes some kind of issues between the kids. His daughters lived next door with JC's parents. He never went to Alta Vista Baptist Church where Grandmother faithfully attended.

Mr. Jolley's name for Uncle David was "Boy."

"Boy" remembers him as "...a heartless, soulless, narcissist. But his big old 1941 Cadillac impressed me."

The only thing worse than taking care of five squirrelly children is taking care of five squirrelly *traumatized* children, which they all had become. Grandmother appeared fearful of what her new husband might think, do, or put up with. It became clear she was ill equipped to handle even the most basic care of the children, much less the stepfamily-related squabbles.

She then picked the child she thought she could handle and added playing favorites to the list of offenses toward her own children. She just kept making bad choices. It seems like all she knew was how to abandon her children. Mr. Jolley was one of those poor choices or perhaps the poor choice was his? She ended up divorcing him only to remarry him and divorce him again.

Grandmother's next choice of a husband was the most dangerous, Mr. King, the one she ran off with shortly after the kids had been released into her care in 1955. They were married in August and the marriage was annulled in October after his murderous assault. I shudder to think of the danger for the children.

She was Mrs. King in August.

She became Mrs. Hale in February of the next year.

That was a good bounce, probably the best of her life. Something should be said for a man like Clifton Hale, who was the fourth and last man Grandmother bounced to.

He became my Papaw. He taught me to rope my golden retriever like he roped cows when he was herding them out west. Cliff served in the army in World War II, landing on Omaha Beach. Yes, he was one of those amazing men. He said that he realized that his backpack was too heavy, so he ditched it all except the two pairs of socks he stuffed in his pockets. He also kept his raincoat. When he landed, a wave picked him up and carried him to shore. A local Lampasas, Texas newspaper reported:

On the beach he met a colonel who had been wounded... he wrapped the man's injured arm and the two of them went over the top to fight together. Cliff literally fought his way to Germany. In the walk from France to Germany, he didn't change clothes for 51 days, and his daily diet consisted of four cigarettes, cheese crackers, a chocolate bar. Sometimes when they were lucky, the soldiers got C rations which included a can of stew and crackers. When the troops reached Germany they were welcomed by more bombings - this time by their own country. They didn't stay outside to watch this time...

Discharged from the army in 1946, he was recalled to serve in the Korean War, this time in the air force.

Apparently highly decorated service in two wars prepared him adequately for marrying my grandmother. Many things good and bad might be said about the other husbands, but it took a lot of something to love Grandmother and keep on loving her while the spicy dynamics of five traumatized children exploded regularly. Many men would have bolted at the first ugly visit. Cliff doubled down, protecting Grandmother.

At the funeral home when we all stood around Grandmother's body. Cliff said, "Look at 'er! She looks like she is just about to sit up and start fussing at me." He loved her and was incomplete without her.

Something should be said for a man like Clifton Hale.

Clifton and Mildred Hale 1960

Clifton and Mildred Hale, 2003

Chapter 29

Scrubbed Clean

Years ago Mom and I visited Houston. She wanted to drive around DePelchin Faith Home. So following her directions I turned down Sandman Street. She changed her mind in a split second and like a terrified child she screamed, "No, no, no! I can't go this way." If she could have, she would have jumped out of the car and run. I could see nothing so horrible, but it was that porch of DePelchin Faith Home, that place where her mother left her and her life came crashing down. The abandonment marked every day of the rest of her life.

Later in 2018, Aunt Sandy and I enter the side, wide entrance that was decorated with bright and pleasant colors. A calm woman with a heavy but kind Hispanic accent met us. Her voice floated between the two languages as she greeted "clients". It was an immaculate office building like a particularly clean doctor's office. The DePelchin Faith Home had become the DePelchin Children's Center focusing on adoption and foster care.

Sandy remembered that one time as a child she was taken to a wealthy woman's home. The lady really liked her and gave her a doll. She wanted to adopt Aunt Sandy, but my grandparents would not relinquish their parental rights. Her parents did not stay her sentence. The kind public relations director at Depelchin Children's Center said that nowadays her parents would not have been given that kind of control.

We walked down the wide hallway passing a large poster: "Stop Child Abuse!" Aunt Sandy chuckled, "I guess it's a little late for us." I didn't have anything within me to accept and process that comment, but there is a place forming in my heart to put all the sadness that I've been learning about. It's a place where it can't derail the rest of my thoughts, my life.

The history wall began with large, dark portraits of important men in the history of DePelchin. Mr Taub, an austere man, looked all business, a wealthy philanthropist. Aunt Sandy whispered like a little girl that Mrs. Taub invited some children to her home. The children rode in the Taub limousine. She took them to have cookies and prunes in her mansion kitchen. Just the kitchen. They weren't allowed anywhere else. Then they returned to Faith Home.

The wall beneath the portrait of Kezia Payne DePelchin read:

> A pioneering teacher, nurse and social worker - took a leap of faith and accepted into her care three orphaned infants for whom no other accommodations were available. Kezia cared for the children in two borrowed rooms at the home of a friend, relying on her personal earnings and donations from compassionate Houstonians. Within a few months on May 2, 1892, Kezia was able to move the children into a small rented house, which she christened 'Faith Home' because she said, "I suppose I will have to call it my 'Faith Home' because I will rely on my faith and God and the good people of Houston to support it. These children must be cared for. We cannot desert them nor fail them.
>
> Kezia died a year later but the Houston community embraced her vision.

Hmm. That is good history.

Our eyes wandered quickly across the years, but I stopped at a photo of a woman holding two babies, surrounded by at least twelve other babies who couldn't have been more than two or three years old. Their little eyes were wide and innocent. What did they do to get those babies to sit still?! I don't want to know. It looked like a photo of a foreign place. That was 1942, when the war brought a huge influx of children needing care.

Aunt Sandy saw it before I did. The photo of happy children wasn't a particularly unusual one except that my mother was in it, right next to Aunt Sandy. Aunt Lena with a large white bow in her hair was on the other end of the row. Aunt Sandy touched the precious photo and wept. She talked and wept. Precious, precious, precious. It is precious to her. The only woman other than my mother who is beautiful when she babbles, babbled on about the photo. There are invisible ribbons to the past that have gently tied her to that spot, that photo, that time, right beside her sister. She couldn't leave so we sat on the bench and waited, eyes wandering back to the picture. Our tour guide, the director of public relations, found us and Aunt Sandy began again, a happy childlike cycle of talking about the photo, the place, her home, her sisters...

But there was no trace of her home... the ravine where they played is still there, but the trees are all new. There is no dining hall, no cottages, no rec. hall. Well maybe one of Aunt Lena's old climbing trees is still there. Maybe.

The road marker, "100 Sandman", and the photo on the wall are all that is left of the Faith Home I have heard about all my life. Always known for being clean, it has now been scrubbed clean of any trace of the days of their childhood. There is no trace of the crushing abandonment that marked five children for the rest of their lives. It seems like there ought to be a monument to the pain endured, the heroics of people working as best they could to help the kids grow up somehow. It seems like it shouldn't be relegated to a history wall and one fuzzy picture for my family.

Aunt Sandy came out of the restroom and said excitedly, "I was just transported back in time by the smell of the cleanser they apparently still use to clean." I was so sorry there wasn't anything left for her. Just so sorry.

Aunt Sandy wasn't sorry though. She was happy to be home, happy to remind the director of public relations of the roots of the organization she works for. She was just happy. That is Aunt Sandy, happy, sweet, charming, beautiful. She seemed to have come to terms with Faith Home, strict and sometimes abusive caregivers, and even her parents' inability to love her in the way that a child needs love.

Aunt Sandy stood smiling by the concrete street sign that says "100 Sandman". It's just a street sign 20 yards from the point of trauma, tragedy, and perhaps salvation from abuse and poverty for many children. So many children were left at that door of DePelchin Faith Home. That compartment in my heart needs to get bigger to take it all in.

Aunt Sandy was still smiling when we said "goodbye" to the public relations director who said, "I'm so glad your experience at DePelchin was so good." We got back into the car and Aunt Sandy said, "I wonder why she said that." I had to laugh. Laughing, smiling children excelling in life equals a good experience. And Aunt Sandy was still smiling.

Abandonment ruins it all for the children.

They may have smiled and laughed but make no mistake: there was nothing positive because when they lost family, they lost everything that counted.

Lena (far left with white bow), Sandra and Dena (second row)

Sandy Bridges 2018

Chapter 30

The Sewage Grate

Aunt Sandy and I set out in her car on probably the very best day ever in Houston: low humidity, cool temperatures, no traffic. We exited the highway and almost immediately we were in the old neighborhood. I smiled to think that the theater Mom and she enjoyed on the weekends was now a Hispanic church. Aunt Sandy stood in one place and pointed to the exact spot the popcorn vendor had sat. She beamingly told me things that my imagination couldn't absorb with the current view of the bare concrete, weeds growing through the cracks, and literally no one in sight. She was so sweet and so happy. I wanted to catch some of that spirit, but I just smiled. I didn't think her joy was sticking yet, but we did have the whole day.

We wandered around the neighborhood to the place she was sure was where their house had been. A fire department had replaced the "perfect home." It was the last place the family lived before DePelchin Faith Home. Aunt Sandy had no idea it wasn't perfect until it was taken away. A large old tree bent its sturdy branches over the edge of the lawn. I would have climbed that tree if I had grown up here. It was disappointing in some ways that nothing was left of the last home the Jody Brooks family resided in together. We walked down the shady lane - really the perfect setting for a family to succeed, just perfect. All of the neighbors houses from that time period still stood with obvious improvements. Just down the street was the Browning Elementary School. Aunt Sandy never stopped talking. We hurried to the front steps where their last family photo had been taken. My grandfather stretched his long lanky legs out holding probably Aunt Jennifer with Grandmother holding baby Uncle David. Momma stood in the back with two large white bows holding her dark hair back and a stuffed animal in her arms. Aunt Lena was also in the back and Aunt Sandy was in front holding her teddy bear and a smile, that I have learned is permanent.

A policeman happened by while she and I were there and offered to take Aunt Sandy's photo in front of the steps. Since the neighborhood is Hispanic I assumed that he was bilingual. He was but the Puerto Rican New York kind of bilingual. He was charmed by Aunt Sandy, as most are. I spoke quietly in Spanish as he took the pictures from different angles. I just wanted him to know he was in the presence of humble greatness, the kind of position you can't obtain but comes only through deep suffering. I didn't elaborate about how she became that way but Aunt Sandy, with the same glowing smile from the 1941 photo, spoke of how she lived here and how wonderful it was until they had to go into DePelchin Faith Home. Yes, he knew DePelchin quite well. He understood.

We passed the fire department one more time and Aunt Sandy said that there used to be a billboard just outside their house with beautiful morning glories all over it. They had taken a family photo there too. I now know why my mother loved morning glories so much. We stood on the street and Aunt Sandy said, " I dropped my teddy bear down that drain and was so sad." I teased her asking her if she would like for me to see if I could find it.

A month later Aunt Sandy called me. She had returned to that spot with her three children and some of their children. She told me excitedly, " I stood on that sewage grate where I lost my teddy bear and realized that the last time I can remember being happy was right there. Right there we were happy, or so I thought. And there I stood again with my family and the happiness I never thought could be." What a sweet spot right over a sewage grate!

Chapter 31

The Kind People

Before we filled out all the paperwork to become foster parents or an adoptive resource for the Department of Social Services in South Carolina, Roger and I carefully considered our purpose for becoming involved. Roger fits the idea of caring for orphans into our calling as Christians. I fit the idea into what my mother needed and lacked. She needed a mother and father without the interference of the government. So in my mind I felt like we should follow Mom's advice and not be involved in fostering at all, but adopt a child who we could perhaps help along the way and provide a soft place to land while she figured life out. After initial visits we would not be entangled in the government system supposedly designed to help children. Roger agreed.

Then we went through training. The training about fostering children was horrendous. Who would want that in their home?! Violence, acting out sexually, stealing, screaming... Nope, not me! We wanted one kid whom we could help, (and I laugh as I write this) for whom we could control some of the environment and influences. How funny that is to think of in hindsight! No one can control much of that at all. Funny. We can't even control much about our own kids. What made me think it would be any different with foster kids?

On our drive home, Roger gingerly broached a topic he knew would rock my way of thinking. He said, "I really think that fostering is more what we are about, in theory. We want to keep families together." Hmm. I agreed with him in theory and rejected the idea that my fifty-plus-year-old self would be any sort of capable of managing fostering as a part of my life. I had seen the videos and couldn't picture myself in any part of it. What about my teenaged kids? Could they be a part of such a thing?

Roger didn't push me. I kind of wondered if he hoped none of this would become part of our lives. We had just moved back to the US from Chile and life was calming down, sort of. Things had been hard for many years and we were enjoying a rest. Fostering or adopting would certainly liven things up.

My biggest problem with fostering was that it seemed like putting a Band-Aid on a femoral bleed. Did it really do any good when death was imminent? Was the kid any different because of time in foster care? I hadn't seen enough successes for it to convince me that it was anything more than a royal headache.

I sometimes play the piano at church even though our church has a band. Sometimes they ask me to play the keyboard when our usual keyboardist is unavailable. For someone trained first as a classical pianist and later as a churchy kind of pianist, playing the keyboard has been quite beneath me. I have remarked that they should get a monkey to come press three keys and hold them down for three measures. Why do they need me? Yes, I am a sometimes-repentant arrogant snob about this, but I still just don't like playing that plastic keyboard with all the buttons when that beautiful baby grand is sitting over there beckoning me to play with what little skill I have left from my ten years of training.

So, after playing that keyboard just a wee bit better than a monkey, I finally decided that it was indeed a different instrument than my beloved piano. I should have probably looked up a tutorial or two about how to play it. Yes, it's a different instrument and I was hardly suited to play it except for knowing where the keys were. The church band didn't need my sense of touch or dexterity. They didn't need my sense of dynamics. The sound guy handled that. They needed musical support with nondescript sounds, bits of piano lines, and some creative accordion sounds mixed with strings. All of it was played without anything more than a page with words and a few chords on it. My respect for our usual keyboard player grew as I tried to figure out how to play this new instrument.

My aversion to foster care was actually a special kind of pride not unlike that snobbery. I didn't want to do it if we would only be remembered by the kid as "those people I had to stay with when they ripped me away from my parents." After all, I am a mother, and family is important. I want my hard-earned recognition as a mother. Besides, I had spent many years figuring this stuff out. I wanted something to show for fostering and, well, there is zero promise for that. Zero. And then there is the thought that we might not be able to do anyone any good. That femoral bleed.

It was my aunts' comments about a certain group of people in their lives when they were wards of the state that helped me pinpoint my role in fostering. Seventy five years later, they talked about "the kind people." Those were people they had short, though sometimes daily, contact with. They still remembered them and the difference they had made, seventy five years later.

The real exposure of my heart came when I realized I didn't want to be just one of the "kind people." I am a mother and I wanted that role. I didn't want to be just a wisp of a memory hanging around in someone's head.

The foster trainer had an insightful comment after one of the potential foster parents asked about dangers involved in foster care. After an hour of answering ridiculous questions, she finally said, "They are children! That's all! Just children!"

Yes, the answers really are so simple.

After talking with my aunts and uncle more I realized I was wrong about the "kind people." being a wisp in their memories. They were so much more. Often times the kind people kept these children from going mad in the midst of a mad, mad, mad, mad world all around them.

I will dedicate the next bit to some of these people who probably remembered the Brooks children until they died, never expecting to receive a medal for their kindnesses. For all the uglies of foster care, there were kind people who looked deep into the souls of these trapped children and tried to help, tried to ease the pain. They tried and they succeeded, and they are remembered in the sweetest wisps of memories which float around whenever these adult children least expect to have a good memory of their childhood. Not tainted with the uglies, they shine and should have at least a few lines each.

Every day Aunt Sandy met Mrs. Priest, the librarian who Aunt Sandy met every day as she left Faith Home. She would beg her to let her and her sisters and friends ride in her car to the next gate and the next one and the next one until she finally had to get out of the car and say "Good-bye." She shared her Suave hand lotion with Aunt Sandy so she could smell good, too.

Momma remembered Cornelia Washington who had soft, brown skin and a sweet smile being, "ever patient with Mrs. McCombs and firm with us if we brought in wet clothes, or muddy feet. The back entrance had a raincoat closet right next to the door. A sink in the boiler room to the right of the back door for cleaning mops, but we could clean shoes there, too."

Cornelia ironed Sunday clothes, someone else pressed others in a cleaner shop next door. Cornelia's role was service but Mom interpreted it as loving service in sharp contrast to Miss McCombs. She wrote of her in several places in her journals.

Raymond "Rags" Ragone was a Drivers Ed teacher at George Washington Junior High School. He was also the Pine Tree Camp Director with his wife, Pinky, and little son, Bo. Aunt Sandy said that one time a bunch of boys grabbed her at school. "You know they think they can do anything they want to you when you are a foster kid and there is no one looking out for you." She told Coach Ragone. He promised her he would deal with it, and he did. The next day the boys walked past her with their heads down. They couldn't even look her in the eye the next day. Coach Rags protected her.

Aunt Lena says, "Alma Johnson was a volunteer who took us to appointments of every kind: doctor, dentist. [We traveled] in a station wagon that Sandy one time leaned against the door [of] and almost fell out." Aunt Sandy says, "I *did* fall out!"

Aunt Sandy also remembers Alma Johnson, "She was not in an office but walking around to see if she could help us or just talk to us. She was one of the ladies who was so sweet to us."

Aunt Jennifer remembers a kind act from Miss Little, the Home Manager. "She gave me a pair of green wedge heeled shoes because we wore the same size."

The college kids who were Pine Tree Camp counselors were so kind to all the kids, playing with them and offering an extra measure of patience just when they needed it.

Aunt Jennifer remembers a couple who cooked at Pine Tree Camp: "Morris and Dorothy lived in a house behind the dining hall and cooked wonderful food. Liked everything but their spaghetti and meat balls because it had Romano cheese."

Most of my aunts remember foster moms who kindly overlooked wet sheets until the kids could stop wetting the bed. It was a kindness not to call attention to the embarrassment.

Aunt Jennifer remembers another example of kindness that she didn't recognize at the time. "You know that foster kids are always craving attention. I always thought my foster mom was mean especially when a brother came and asked me to sit on his lap and she wouldn't let me. I didn't know he was a 'funny uncle.' She was protecting me."

Sometimes there were good caseworkers like Dieter Geoff, Uncle David's last caseworker. "He listened to me. He was nice to me. The others didn't seem interested in me. I heard from him while I was in the navy."[7]

Aunt Sandy says, "A Jewish couple would come to the home and take as many kids as they could get into the car. When we would get out in downtown Houston people would count how many kids got out."

Something should be said about the kind people who intentionally entered into the place of pain for the children. Perhaps they were just doing their jobs, but they chose to work at a children's home. They chose to smile and give much needed caresses. They chose to protect. They couldn't stop the femoral bleed but they did what they could, and it helped. Even today it helps.

Chapter 32

Joe Euresti and Others

The Brooks siblings weren't the only children at Faith Home. There were many other kids who resided there. For some it was home for a little while. For others, it was the only home they had ever known.

Aunt Sandy's friend list begins with Frances Jones who was known for being a bad influence. JoAnn McBee was a close friend until she passed away. Marie Brocato was a friend for a short while until she was adopted into a wealthy family. Aunt Sandy was able to visit her once. Skippy Eaves was a friendly boy. Lemuel Gilbert was also nice and tried to date Aunt Sandy, but she was going with someone else. Robert Hall was a nice older boy.

Lillian Coranza, Millie and Tillie Euresti were some of the older girls who jitterbugged with Momma. Mary Ann Musgrove was known for being beautiful.

Some thrived, like David Powell, Birdie Green and Joe Euresti.

"We all loved David Powell. He carried me when I won best camper. He later became a professor at a university in Mexico. He was also a counselor at Pine Tree Camp," Aunt Sandy says.

Birdie Green also excelled in Faith Home. Momma talked about Birdie.

Joe Dell Euresti came to Faith Home under much different circumstances. He came with his two sisters, Millie and Tillie, who were teased when the other children learned that Mrs. Euresti had sewn underwear into their clothes. That sounds like a smart mother to me!

Joe said, "My mother was to have a gall bladder surgery operation and we were to stay at DePelchin Faith Home for six to nine months until she recovered… After a few weeks, I remembered my Dad picking us up from DePelchin. I thought we were finally going home. He drove us in his pickup away from the orphanage… He told us our mother had gone to Heaven and we were to remain at Faith Home. Our mother died during the gallbladder operation due to kidney failure at Herman Hospital. I cried for days. They had to call my sisters to come and console me…It took more than a few days for me to stop crying."

Somehow Joe was able to look past his own pain and give even more to those around him. That is a rare gift indeed.

His obituary said, "Joe was known as a happy man, always fun to be around, dancing his way into the room. He loved to dance…" He was also the first child from DePelchin Faith Home that got to go to college.

Joe seemed to flourish. He was the most likable guy, known and loved by everyone at Faith Home from the day he entered, until his death in 2019. He remained in contact with Faith Home and became known as Papa Joe to everyone. Joe accepted everybody as they were and always had a smile on his face.

Joe surely was a bright spot at Faith Home. I wish I could have met Papa Joe.

Joe Euresti

Joe Euresti and David Powell

Chapter 33

Reprieve?

I have left so much out! My aunts and uncle would say I really missed the mark of how special some things about DePelchin were. It was indeed special with a hefty price tag for all the benefits. The full truth it is all too hard to think about and digest. Too heavy.

There has to be a break or a relief.

I breezed over my notes again to be sure there wasn't something sweet I could write about that would give us all a break from remembering sad things. We can only grieve so long, right?

I tried to put myself in the children's shoes.

Did they giggle anyway? They were just children who do what children do.

They had no reprieve. Abandonment never left them, never let up the suffocating pressure it exerted on them. It told them all kinds of lies that no one can un-tell. So why should there be a reprieve for us?

Well, there was a reprieve. There was a lovely reprieve that I almost missed entirely.

Sandy at Pine Tree Camp

Chapter 34

Pine Tree Camp

I have heard of Pine Tree Camp all of my life, but never thought much about it. It was a camp. Whatever could be so important about a summer camp? Oh but I should have listened better! It was so much more than summer fun!

My aunts chatter on about their summer camp experience. I had a summer camp experience that was pretty wonderful, but it isn't something I talk about now as an adult. They do. They still sing the songs and glow when they remember the campfires and marshmallows.

I am beginning to understand some of what the kids endured in the institution. So let me see if I can do justice to the only reprieve and break Faith Home kids got.

School let out. They counted the days until the bus took them to Spring, Texas to Pine Tree Camp singing all the way and even more the closer they got to the camp:

> *When all the Pine Tree Campers fall in line,*
> *We're gonna have a happy and joyous time.*
> *From early morn until the sun departs,*
> *We're gonna run and swim and play with*
> *All our hearts.*
> *You're gonna see how much we love our camp,*
> *Our Faith Home counselors and campers too.*
> *For every hour spent with you, all of you,*
> *At Pine Tree Camp!*

My aunts, looking like little girls on a bus to camp, began singing that song in my kitchen. I did have the good sense to pull out my phone and record those sweet eighty-year-old ladies singing!

The kids looked forward to the camp all year! It was their saving grace getting them briefly out of Faith Home where everything was so structured. They felt like birds in a cage, and Pine Tree Camp was a little flight out in the woods to stretch their wings.

The following are little bits that Aunt Jennifer and Aunt Sandy told me about Pine Tree Camp. Picture two little girls jumping up and down, telling you about this camp. That is what I saw as these two senior ladies recounted Pine Tree Camp. They don't jump up and down physically anymore, but they would if they could!

"It was the best! …A month of freedom. I got to go twice. I got to go when the little kids went and I got to go when the big girls went because I had older sisters. At first when we went to the camp, they had tents on a wooden platform, and we loved those tents. Then they moved to cabins with canvass windows. Tents were more fun. Campfires every night and showers in another building. After campfire, the fastest runners got the warm water and the rest got cold showers. And I always got to be in the right place with people who ran fast.

"Watermelon fights around the campfire. We made up radio shows: 'Soggies, the brand new cereal. It doesn't snap, it doesn't crackle, it doesn't pop. It just lays in the bowl and sops up all the milk.'

"One summer I was archery champion! I was also best camper at the end of the month! That was a good year! Winning 'Best Camper' is a trophy still treasured. "David Powell [apparently Camp Pine Tree heart throb] carried me piggyback.

"They had movies and then at the end ran the movie backwards.

"At camp, we played baseball, horseshoes, old fashioned archery, swimming…I learned to dive with my feet about eight inches from the edge…more fun…and we loved to swim underwater the length of the pool!

"We went on long hikes where the counselors would point out the different snakes to us such as a king, pygmy, water moccasins. I remember one time a counselor caught a coral snake and pointed out to us red and yellow kill a fellow. I never forgot that.

"Some nights we'd have amateur night. Dena, Lena, and I sang I *Can't Begin to Tell You*- a Betty Grable song. Can't remember if we won…probably not. Ha. But, we did sing good together.

"One time, the lady counselors took us hiking and we spent the night there beside the creek. We had baked potatoes in the fire. Roasted marshmallows. Later we swam naked in the creek…fun!

"We used to jump off that high bridge at the lower end into the white sand along the river. We slept in our clothes.

"Oh, I remember, too, going hiking and finding an old abandoned cabin in the woods. Fun looking in, and some things were just like they used to be.

"We would eat wild muscadine grapes off the vines in the woods.

Those eighty-year-old campers still glow like fireflies when they talk about Pine Tree Camp. I was incredulous just watching them talk about it! I didn't want to crush their fun, but I certainly wanted to know what made this camp so special. It didn't seem connected to that moment when they first crossed the bridge and entered the camp, or the cabins or the scenery, though it was indeed beautiful! So what was so great about Pine Tree Camp?!

It was a place of reprieve from Faith Home. It was a place that promised that perhaps, just perhaps, their entire lives would not be ruled by whatever grief and loss brought them into what often seemed like oppressive care within DePelchin Faith Home.

Pine Tree Camp was the exact opposite of the Home. There was no confinement. The counselors loved on the kids unconditionally, nothing was negative. It was heaven to kids who desperately needed a little bit of relief.

I questioned Aunt Jennifer very closely on this matter. "So there was absolutely nothing negative about Pine Tree Camp??"

"Nothing."

" How about abuse? Any abusive counselors?"

"No! It was wonderful wonderful wonderful!"

"How about kids misbehaving or getting into trouble?"

"Well, there was this little thing or that, but no trouble! None!"

I might add that there were no parents around bringing with them the sometimes painful dynamics that came with visits.

Pine Tree Camp was… perfect.

They sat around the campfire on logs singing into the evening…

"Green trees around you,

blue skies above,

friends all around you in a world filled with love,

taps sounding softly,

hearts beating true,

As we all sing goodnight to you….

Day is done,

gone the sun,

from the lakes, from the hills, from the sky.

All is well, safely rest,

God is nigh."

Chapter 35

Dena

Momma and Daddy called me in Chile in December of 2011. Daddy had suffered with Parkinson's for some time, but the latest diagnosis was very serious. They wanted us to know. He had inoperable kidney cancer. His doctor always told him that something else would probably get him before Parkinson's. This was it. There would be no treatment, and he only had a short time left, perhaps months. He was already so thin.

We moved our travel plans to the US up by several weeks. Bringing a family of six back to the US for an indefinite period is a complicated matter. Our oldest daughter would graduate high school in May of 2012, in the US so we came a little early, arriving in early April. We tried to help Momma and Daddy, but we weren't much use, except that Momma smiled a lot. She donned her famous bandana and took the children outside to walk in the wet spring grass. I walked and talked with the most contented Momma I had ever seen. She was exhausted, but she was happy and content. Smiles came easily on her relaxed face. At one point she had that furrowed brow that I had seen all my life. It usually meant she was struggling with guilt, so I began my usual speech. It was rather long, but started something like this:

"Though your sins were as scarlet, they shall be white as snow… For as far as the east is from the west, so far have I removed your transgressions…"

She stopped me before I could get too far into it. Laughing, she said, "I don't think I need to hear that this time. I think God just wants me to know that He is my Father."

Aunt Jennifer came to town to help us celebrate Mom's seventy-fifth birthday on April 20. I lit the whole Scrabble cake up with candles. We sang and laughed. On Friday Momma was so tired. Her blood pressure was low. I made a mental note to mention it to the doctor on Monday. We never got to Monday.

I sat with Daddy on Sunday so that Momma could go to church. She showed off her new shoes at church and hurried home. I had a picnic in the afternoon to attend, so I hugged her and hugged her again just because I loved her and waltzed out the door to my event. I should have hugged her one more time.

Daddy called me at about 1:00 am. He couldn't awaken Momma. I drove the thirty-minute drive in twenty, thinking that she was just sleeping heavily, and Daddy needed help as he often did. My cousin, Deevy, met me in the driveway. He told me she was gone and caught me as I collapsed. She was gone, a massive something…

The funeral home in our small town was surprised as they had been expecting Daddy, not Momma. They came and took her precious body. Daddy and I sat staring at each other, but the house was inexplicably calm, filled with the "hesed" love of God that had told Momma that He was her father and had given her contentment. I never could have imagined being comforted as we were that night. God had been kind to Momma. For all the things in her life that she had suffered, she would not suffer another blow of abandonment as

Daddy would soon be leaving this life. She was even more than content now than a few days earlier.

Momma passed away April 23, 2012 and Daddy lingered another two months, passing away on June 23, 2012.

Momma's passing jolted the community, who was quite aware of Daddy's condition. I can't really say what the jolt was like for Aunt Lena, Aunt Sandy, Aunt Jennifer, and Uncle David. It never mattered that they were separated by many miles, states, differences of opinions, or anything. They had each other, and that mattered. It was a gut punch for all, too soon. Momma was the first to go and it was too soon.

Momma left the impression of her love all over her children. By treasuring us as every child should be treasured, Momma changed our DNA and perhaps the DNA of generations to come. She wasn't supposed to be able to, but she did it. "Grateful" doesn't begin to describe how I feel about it.

CHAPTER 36

Rage, Grace and Mercy

Funny how the love of a mother and father invisibly gives children everything that they need to succeed. The opposite is also true. Losing it cripples them, maims them for life. I can't fathom the abandonment and how that crippled these children, although I have certainly tried.

If love is measured in pain suffered my grandparents loved their children deeply. They hurt immensely as their immature selves weathered the storm of losing the kids. But their own wounds seemed to take precedence over the suffering of their children. It must have been overwhelming pain to blind them to their own children.

My accusing finger points and shakes. I myself would never have done such a thing. Never.

It's easier than you would think to overlook our own faults. I don't admit my selfish mistakes of motherhood any more than my grandmother did. While the children's brains were being rewired to accept abandonment, the parents were telling themselves that it wasn't that bad. They weren't guilty. It's the children who bear the brunt of the lies we tell ourselves.

Like all illnesses, I just hope and pray that my selfishness is the garden variety cold and not the ravaging cancer of abandonment. We are all capable of every vice. We are all susceptible to all human weakness. No one is immune.

I didn't realize how badly this story needed to be told until I started writing. Telling this story has been like putting together a shattered vase. The lines of glue still show and there are missing pieces, lots of missing pieces. Perhaps just the attempt to bring the pieces together is an expression of the deep love I have for five siblings who endured what no person should ever have to endure.

Aunt Jennifer said, "Here I am at almost eighty and I see myself at five years old and I begin to cry because after all these years I want to believe it didn't happen, but it did."

I didn't really tell the whole truth in these few pages. It was much worse than I alluded to, but you figured that out. I still become enraged thinking about it, but rage only escalates pain and suffering. Grace and mercy? It soothes and heals where rage inflames.

In 1998 we bought two little beds for our two oldest children, five and three years old. They snuggled down under the comforters and used the beds for years. They passed the beds along to their younger brother and sister who also snuggled down under the comforter on many cold nights. There are scratches on the side of one and some of the wooden slats that support the mattresses are broken from children jumping on beds that can't endure jumping. Little Girl snuggled down under the quilts while I duct-taped the offending shade to the window frame because it scared her. "Big Momma" who was actually rather small, snuggled down under the blankets with all the things she hoarded beneath her pillow that she didn't know I knew about. Then there was a sister and brother whose mother passed away unexpectedly leaving 6 children behind. They crawled into the beds exhausted from losing their Momma and caring for younger siblings all day. I piled the quilts high on them even on a warm fall evening and turned the air conditioner to ice cold so that they could sleep under the comforting weight. They didn't know that they would all be adopted together before Christmas.

It's time to put the beds into storage. I will take them apart for the first time tomorrow... or maybe not. Maybe there is a little spot in the office I can put them just in case God gives me the opportunity to look into those brown eyes, those dark green eyes, those clear blue eyes that blink away the tears and confusion. Maybe I will be given the opportunity to absorb the pain of a child again and put her or him to sleep with:

"Father we thank Thee for the night and for the pleasant morning light. For rest and food and clothes we wear, and all that makes the world so fair. Amen."

Grace and mercy... Maybe I can be one of the "kind people."

Made in the USA
Middletown, DE
13 December 2021